Architectural Styles

Architectural Styles
Herbert Pothorn

A Studio Book The Viking Press   *New York*

Baustile © Südwest Verlag GmbH & Co. KG, Munich, 1968
English-language translation Copyright © 1970 by B. T. Batsford Ltd

Published in 1971 by the Viking Press, Inc.
625 Madison Avenue, New York, N.Y. 10022
SBN 670–13100–8
Library of Congress catalog card number: 77–101774
Printed and bound in Great Britain by Jarrold and Sons Ltd, Norwich

Contents

Reconstruction of the Temple of Victory on the Acropolis, Athens; built by Callicrates in the Ionic order, *c.* 420 B.C.

Introduction

This book will allow the interested layman, without knowing any of the technical terms, to review the character and significance of architectural change throughout the ages. As much detail as possible has been gathered together in fewer than 200 pages — little enough when we think of the amount of material available, which covers more than 5,000 years, but enough to show the logical continuity.

The history of building styles is the history of the change in man's search for protection, comfort, decoration and individuality. As far as we are concerned, the last of these is the most important since it is through striving for individuality that a style is created. A roof covering, a sleeping place and a hearth is not architecture, nor is a sacrificial altar under a tree. As soon as any other consideration than use enters into construction we have the dawn of style From these beginnings we trace the story through many periods and many countries to the present day.

It will become clear that the great variety of materials and opportunities at the disposal of the present-day architect makes his task both simpler and more difficult. But it will also become clear that regrets for vanished splendours are no more justified than they have ever been.

Stone statuette (about nine inches high) found on one of the Cyclades islands in the Aegean; probably *c*. 3000 B.C.

Materials and Tools

Primitive man must have soon found the natural cave inadequate and to improve it he probably dug and levelled the floor, laid flagstones, covered them with sand, or clay, and stamped it down firmly. This was his first step in building.

For practical reasons the caveman usually built his fireplace near the entrance, or in the middle foreground, of his cave. To do this he laid a semicircle of stones and then, seeing that flat stones could be placed on top of each other, would pile them up. The interstices, which could not be called joints yet, he would fill with clay. The fire, burning continuously, baked the clay remarkably hard — so the hearth came into being. In the dark background of the cave, sleeping quarters were made of straw and animal skins, and it proved better to prepare this soft bed about two feet above the ground on a bank of stones against the wall. Thus the sleepers would be pro-

tected from damp, and this stone shelf would provide more comfortable seating than the flat ground during the day.

The first dwelling was by no means a building or a house. The effort required to fashion it from the given material was slight. What had to be done could be done with the hands and feet and, perhaps, a stick for digging. The inhabitants would feel no regrets if the shelter had to be abandoned for another which promised better hunting, a sunnier slope or was closer to a stream.

It is possible that the small masonry hearth became the model for the first house. The walls surrounded the hearth at a distance of two arm spans on either side. Above a depression one span wide and two spans deep, the walls afforded protection to the whole family. The roof was made of branches, twigs and sheaves of straw but, if little wood was available, other forms of roof structure were developed, even in the earliest times.

The first builders only needed to overlap the walling stones for the enclosed space to become narrower towards the top. In this way a pointed vault rose over the substructure, no matter whether this was square, oblong or round. The builders needed only to consider how many sleepers were going to use the house — the form of the roof became inevitable, walls and roof were one entity.

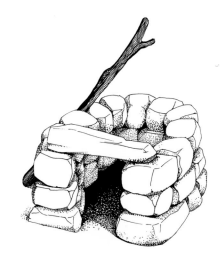

Stone Age hearth

The whole building could be erected virtually without tools, since the stones for such a house did not require much shaping, given sufficient time to try out which stones would fit best. A 'ladder', consisting of a framework of branches, could be piled up quickly when the rising vaulting could no longer be reached from the ground.

It must have been quickly discovered that one stone could be used to shape or split another and that by using this idea a building could be made better, tidier and more beautiful. With the improvement of the tool, there would also come the improvement of building techniques and the use of the particular characteristics of the materials involved; horizontal joints would be made as horizontal as possible, vertical joints — and the builders would discover this quickly — would have to be staggered from one course to the next to give walls greater stability. Then builders would start taking care to construct walls without bulges or irregularities, and projecting sharp edges, especially those on inner walls, would be smoothed out. The first clumsy masonry masses would be transformed into smooth walls.

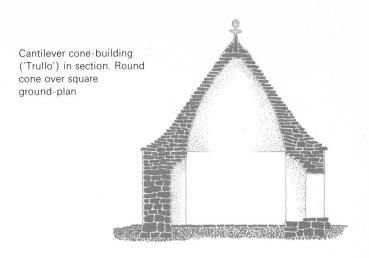

Cantilever cone-building ('Trullo') in section. Round cone over square ground-plan

Terraced Trulli — a row of houses in Alberobello, Apulia, Italy

Style Without Plan

From the simplest rules an architectural order arose, not according to a plan but by natural growth. Over a square ground-plan rising walls could be narrowed, course by course, so that they approximated to a circular form. This led to a cone over square walls, with a smoke-vent at the top. For houses without a hearth this vent could be sealed with a stone, or with a shaped cap of clay that could take any form that occurred to the builder — a boss, a convex cap, a double horn, a pine cone or a cross.

Thus an early style arose, coarse in features, not pursued too intently, not particularly beautiful, yet indicative of future developments and maintained to this day in remote districts.

9

Round huts of stone and clay at Khirokitia, Cyprus
(reconstruction and section)

and Gothic styles. Compared with this castle the Trulli are interesting trifles, yet moving and venerable in their gaucheness.

None of the Trulli still standing in Apulia have survived from the Stone Age but the building principle involved has and can be found, modified, in many parts of the Mediterranean. Near Khirokitia in Cyprus excavations have revealed the remains of forty-eight stone huts which are undoubtedly prehistoric. Round buildings, close together, partly furnished with sleeping quarters on a raised platform — the remains of a small community which existed more than 7,000 years ago.

Of a much later date are the stone cone-huts to be found in Alpine countries and in Provence. As might be expected they are by no means standardized — square, oval, circular shapes exist, even in one district.

Many of these buildings were first discovered by tourists who passed and were surprised at what they thought must be 'very old' buildings. They certainly looked archaic, almost prehistoric, especially those in a state of disrepair and those which have not been altered since they were built. But appearances can be deceptive.

On the high Alpine pastures at Sassal Masone, near the Bernina Pass, there were two fine cone-huts by the roadside. These were thought to be from the early Middle Ages or even earlier. But Hans Soeder, an architect from Darmstadt, discovered that they were built after 1870. He found the grandson of the builder, who told him that his grandfather was a pastrycook from Italy. With his servant, whom he had brought from a valley near Bergamo, he had built the two stone huts and had used them as an inn. There had been a third cone above a milk-cellar, but this had been torn down when the cellar became too small for the business.

Of course no one in Alberobello today will go to a builder and say, 'Build me a Trullo.' He will probably want a house of 'patent' cement stones built on a concrete base — for his money he can demand something modern. The first person that did this in Alberobello must have received something quite exotic, for around him dwelt families in their inherited Trulli. True, they had been renewed countless times, improved, plastered and lime-washed inside and out, and had glazed windows and electric light, but the stone cone-roofs were not disturbed, either with added chimneys or even with television aerials. Two hours' car journey north-west of the Apulian Trullo-villages stands Castel del Monte, the hunting lodge of the Hohenstaufen emperor, Frederick II, a lonely towering harmony of Romanesque, Oriental

Clay model of a house, excavated from a grave near Strelitz in Moravia, from about 2000 B.C.

Circle and Square

No purpose is served by wondering which of the two fundamental forms, the square or the circle, is the older, and whether one developed from the other. The circle recalls the cave, but it cannot be assumed that it is the prototype. It has the advantage that it encloses the greatest possible area with the smallest amount of material; but that is a reflection which pre-supposes a knowledge of geometry. It would be more obvious to deduce the idea of the circle from the enclosure formed by the protective walls round the depression which was the floor of the first hut.

The square corresponds to the spatial needs of a recumbent human being. Two or more beds placed side by side produce a rough square and when the builders began to add one square space to another the angles between the walls would remain constant. Thus the centre lines, the axes of the square buildings, remain perpendicular to each other — corresponding to a human being standing ready to move, looking in the direction of his first step, whose outstretched arms would indicate the second axis at right angles to the first.

The building material of early times — the unhewn stone — is just as adaptable to either form, the circle (and its related polygonal forms, the hexagon and the octagon) or the square. Wood as a building material produces a wall composed of straight lines, since it cannot be bent or rounded to suit a purpose. Therefore a Trullo or Provençal shepherd's hut cannot be made of wood. Yet wood is the accepted material for the roof, which rests on the walls of the house as an independent component. The roof, either steep or gentle, can sit like a saddle over the ridge-piece, or rise like a pyramid as a so-called 'tent-roof'. It can project, to protect the walls of the house from snow and rain, or, in the form of a loggia, can furnish a covered space for sitting outside. From the beginning, wood required tools for its preparation, unlike the early stone construction.

The improvement of tools meant that materials could be put to the best use, both technically and stylistically, for the flowering of the craftsman's art naturally increases his mastery over the materials used, but it also increases the desire to do justice to the wood or to the stone and therefore to the craftsman's taste. An idea will sprout from nowhere. From the idea a plan will develop — not yet on 'paper' with all its details, but nevertheless a thought-out anticipation of the building explained with a few strokes in the sand.

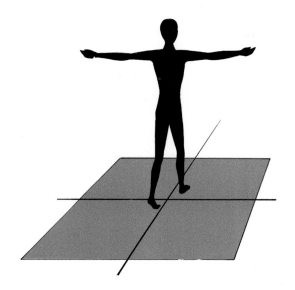

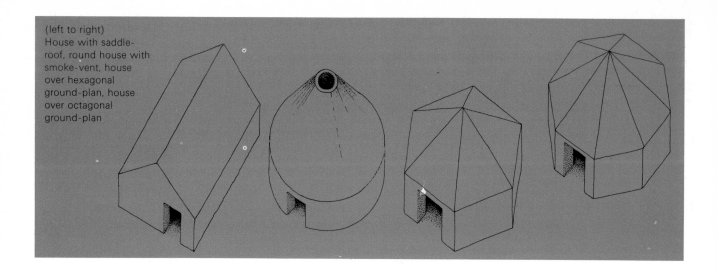

(left to right)
House with saddle-roof, round house with smoke-vent, house over hexagonal ground-plan, house over octagonal ground-plan

It is only at this point that we can talk of style as the result of a spiritual or intellectual attitude, which involves imagination no less than mastery of the materials. These two factors combine to elevate the work above the everyday level and make it inherently comprehensible. Style is always the fusion of intellectual, spiritual, technical and economic potentialities. If that sounds too abstract at least it is brief.

And yet these four factors are not enough. For the creation of architecture something has to come from outside — an inspiration which cannot be explained except with metaphors and circumlocutions like 'creative spark' or 'flash of insight', which do not get near the heart of the matter. These words can only remain phrases, they do not explain how it happens that at certain periods the creative spark is kindled by something which eludes the understanding.

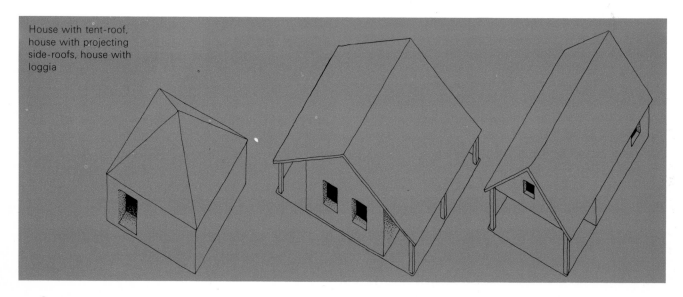

House with tent-roof, house with projecting side-roofs, house with loggia

The square, the polygon, the circle; stone, wood, clay; brick, cement, metal; glass, stucco, paint; these are the constituents that go to make up a style. But they are powerless without the spark, without the inspiration, without that 'something in the air', which brings about a work of art.

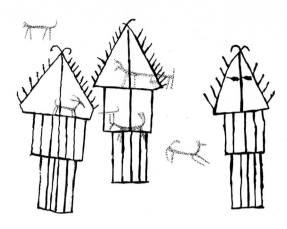

Primitive representation of wooden houses, probably lake dwellings. Rock drawings from Val Camonica in northern Italy, apparently from about the second millennium B.C.

Arch and Cupola

In many regions of the world, wherever it was necessary for man to protect his hearth and his sleeping quarters against cold, snow and rain, or against heat, buildings have grown up similar to the houses of Khirokitia in Cyprus or to the coned roofs of Apulia. In the Sudan a mixture of clay and chaff is used to build them. The Eskimos use snow stamped into blocks for their igloos. The Navaho Indians built domed winter huts of turfs placed over a scaffolding of poles.

Many attempts have been made to solve the puzzle of why similar buildings were constructed independently in all parts of the world. There are mysterious explanations: the longing for security which is perfectly satisfied by the circular form as in a cave, in an egg, in the womb. It is possible that such feelings played an unconscious part. More cogent, however, would be the fact that by trial and error a form had been found which was technically sound and relatively easy to construct.

These radial forms were not real domes or vaults, and to distinguish them from genuine ones they are called cantilever-vaults. They occur because of the circular overlapping of the stones following the decrease in diameter from course to course. The joints are as horizontal as possible; the stones as flat and as large as possible.

The genuine vault stems from complicated considerations which require that the stones be accurately worked on all four sides since the joints are no longer horizontal but are aligned radially to the centre of the arch's curvature.

It is not possible to build the vault freely as with a cantilever-vault. Before building begins interior scaffolding has to be erected so that the stones do not fall down during construction, since the vault — whether arch, barrel or cupola — is not firm and stable until it is finished. But then the vaulting spans a space whose height and breadth would not have been possible by the old building methods. Careful planning and exact measurements are prerequisites, for the stability of the building depends upon the exactness of the vaulting and the constancy of the curvature.

The technology for building the arch and vault originated in the East. By the year 2000 B.C. it was

13

general throughout the Middle East and had reached an astonishing degree of perfection. In spite of their early contacts with the East neither the ancient Egyptians nor the Greeks were interested in the vault. They both erected roofs over their 'post and lintel' walls — a building method which originated from the use of wood but which was soon adapted in various ways to stone, the posts becoming columns in all their stylistic variations and the lintels, the architrave. Around 300 B.C. the technique of the rounded arch was taken up by the Romans, and since then it has never been discarded in Western building.

Besides stone and brick the Romans used a new material which was particularly suitable for the round arch — concrete. In Palestrina, the old Praeneste, stand the ruins of the Temple of Fortune which was built in the third century B.C. It was a colossal building with a series of barrel-vaults in two storeys that were constructed by pouring concrete over a mould. The concrete consists of rubble pieces, about as big as a man's hand, held together with a natural cement of volcanic ash. Building in concrete is not, therefore, a 'modern' method of construction as one sometimes reads but, equally, it was not discovered by the Romans. In volcanic districts it was known and widely used, in early antiquity. On the Aeolian islands, north of Sicily, the remains of concrete buildings have been discovered which were built before 1500 B.C. and were constructed of rubble, volcanic ash and water.

In the older literature on the history of art, volcanic cement is not mentioned. It was barely noticed by the classical scholars, although the building charac-teristics of Praeneste could scarcely be overlooked. The interest in quality and form seems to have been greater than the desire to examine the technical and working methods of past epochs. Moreover, the concrete walls of the volcanic islands seem to have been discovered later and it is only recently that they could be accurately dated.

Early Antiquity

Drawing, after a portrait study of a king's head, probably Amenophis IV, Echnaton, *c.* 1360 B.C.

Egypt

The earliest culture which influenced Europe came from the Nile – after it had flowered there for 2,000 years and was in decline after the extinction of its last dynasty. The Greeks and the Phoenicians traded with Egypt. Towards the end of the sixth century B.C. came the Persians, who ruled as a foreign power for over 100 years. In 332 Alexander the Great made Egypt a part of his empire, ruling over it as 'the divine son of Amun'. After him the Ptolemies ruled, a dynasty founded by the Macedonian Ptolemy, which in spite of six brother-sister marriages was never a Macedonian family but a mixture of Egyptian, Libyan, Nubian and Syrian blood. The last of this line was Cleopatra, who literally fell at the feet of Caesar.

The Romans made Egypt the granary of their empire and admitted the Nile gods to their Pantheon. In Roman times the stylistic influence of Egypt on the cultures of the Mediterranean gradually ceased and the closed portals of the royal tombs, which for so long had resisted the incursions of time, no longer earned the reverence of the desert tribes which penetrated into the upper Nile valley. What modern archaeologists have recovered from the few tombs left untouched by robbers is, in spite of its apparent abundance, only the shadow of departed greatness, preserved because of fear of the afterlife.

In 1799 one of Napoleon's lieutenants found under a ruined house in the delta the basalt slab which later became famous as the Rosetta Stone. This stone contains the same text chiselled in hieroglyphics, in Greek and in an Egyptian popular alphabet. In 1822 the French achaeologist Jean-François Champollion succeeded in partly deciphering the other two texts from the Greek one, an event which is regarded as the birth of scientific research in the Nile valley.

Since that date Egyptian history has been rewritten. With the help of the text it was possible to form a firm conception of the nature of Egyptian buildings – until then only surmised – and of their relationship to the cosmos and to the beyond.

The audacious scale of these buildings was an awesome expression of royal power, and to the peasant by the river it was an assurance of the divine origin of all kings from time immemorial. Who but a god could have transported so many great stones? Moved mountains?

With the exception of the works created for subduing the Nile floods, the art of building was only at the

15

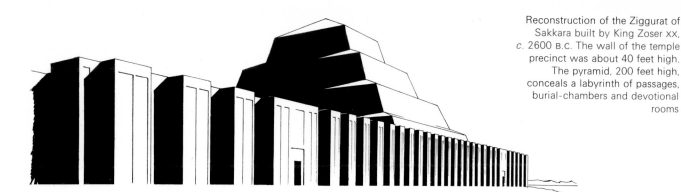

Reconstruction of the Ziggurat of Sakkara built by King Zoser xx, *c.* 2600 B.C. The wall of the temple precinct was about 40 feet high. The pyramid, 200 feet high, conceals a labyrinth of passages, burial-chambers and devotional rooms

service of kings, of gods and of the dead. Naturally there were granaries, archives and military installations, but the architectural resources involved were small compared to the royal buildings.

The king owned all quarries in the rock-valleys, and he was master of an army of slaves. But this does not explain the gigantic scale of his buildings, nor was it a matter of chance. It was the result of a self-imposed task to build a model of the spatial and temporal structure of a universe in which the Nile valley was the centre.

In the third millennium B.C. the star Alpha Draconis revolved round the celestial pole with a deviation of less than three degrees. In turn the rest of the fixed-star sky seemed to revolve, night by night, round it. In lower Egypt this polar star of the pharaonic age stood at 33 degrees above the horizon. This angle can be seen in the inclined shafts which lead to burial-chambers in the Pyramids. The sides of the Cheops Pyramid, which are exactly aligned to the four points of the compass, have an angle of inclination of 52

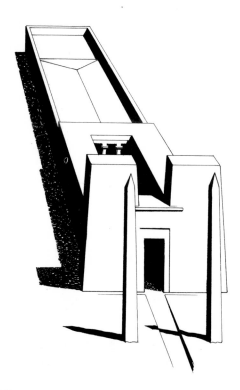

Reconstruction of a temple-complex. The outer walls are unjointed; the façade is covered with pictograms. Buildings of this kind were also built into rock-walls (as Abu Simbel). The rooms always lie one behind the other along a middle axis in an east—west direction

16

degrees. This corresponds to the zenith of the fixed star, Sothis, which we call Sirius.

The measurement of the circumference of the base of the Cheops Pyramid discloses a relationship to the length of the sun-year. The Egyptian builders had a unit of measurement which present-day archaeologists call the pyramid-metre (equals 2 feet 1 inch). One twenty-fifth of a pyramid-metre is one pyramid-inch. At its base the length of the Cheops Pyramid is approximately 250 yards. The exact length can no longer be determined as the facing of the stones has disappeared. But if one assumes a length of something under 254 yards and converts it into Egyptian measurements then the circumference of the pyramid measures 36,524 pyramid-inches. This figure corresponds to the length of the sun-year with 365·24 days — up to the second decimal place; thus the Cheops Pyramid has measurements which are related both spatially and temporally to astronomical values.

This pyramid offers an impressive proof of the mathematical-astronomical knowledge of the period; also of the expense involved. For in order to build it 100,000 labourers had to work for 20 years to pile up 2½ million blocks of stone each with an average weight of 50 cwt.

Almost every edifice in ancient Egypt, whether rock-grave, pyramid-grave or temple, was built to plans in which astronomical calculations played as large a part as aesthetic motives. The desire for imposing display finally determined the form, and it is understandable that the impression on the people was a mixture of wonder and uneasiness. Spacious façades stand guard over forests of columns forming mysterious courts which only a few initiated were allowed to enter. The walls were bedecked with picture writing which hardly anyone could read. Pharaoh in his might could no longer be comprehended by the simpler creatures of earth.

In the long history of Egyptian building the variations of style are slight. There are temple façades, such as those in Karnak and in Edfus, which are similar in principle and in detail, yet which in their completion are separated by 1,000 years. Once the form had been determined it remained the correct style for all time.

Section through the Cheops Pyramid. The king's chambers are in the middle, above those of the queen

Two examples of Egyptian column-orders, stylized from plant models: on the left, papyrus; on the right, lotus

The colossal statues at the entrance to the temple at Abu Simbel, hewn out of the rock under Rameses II, 1290–1223 B.C. In order to save the edifice from the rising waters of the Nile after the completion of the Aswan Dam, it was transported in 1964–7 to a secure position and rebuilt much higher than its former site

Repetition was a symbol of permanence.

For each pharaoh the building of his tomb was the great theme of his life, and if he were granted a long, peaceful reign the work took on gigantic proportions. It often happened that the tomb was enlarged by his successor because the chambers could not contain all the treasures which were bestowed on the dead king for his journey into the other world. We know that in ancient Egypt the preoccupation with death and the beyond was universal, but for the cult as it pertained to the dead of the humbler social classes there is as little evidence as to their way of life.

A text written in one royal tomb gives us a hint of the chasm between the mighty and the humble:

> 'Those who hewed these hard stones, who worked to build this beautiful hall into the pyramid, who erected the stone obelisk, their places of sacrifice are as empty as those of the weary ones who die on the banks of the Nile, and no one commemorates them.'

The inscription for the king reads:

> 'Heaven's portals stand open for you, the heavy bolts are withdrawn. The sun-god takes you by the hand and leads you and sets you on the throne of Osiris, the master of the dead. You do what he does. You enable your house to flourish after you and you protect your children with care.'

In January 1960 President Nasser of Egypt pressed a button to explode ten tons of dynamite, thereby inaugurating the building of the new Aswan Dam. This dam, on its completion, would cause the water-level of the Nile to rise over 300 feet and make the river overflow its old banks for a stretch of over 250 miles. This meant that the tombs and temples between Aswan (Philae) and Wadi Halfa would have been lost for ever had not Unesco successfully initiated a world-wide appeal for the rescue and removal of the old monuments which, with a few exceptions, were moved and re-erected in secure positions under the guidance of expert archaeologists.

Drawing after a wall-painting in the fortress of Tiryns; noble lady with a sacrifice

The Aegean

At a time when in Egypt hardly a stone was used in construction which had not been geometrically thought out, in the Peloponnese, on the Aegean islands and in Crete the walls of buildings were rough, as if the large stones had been carelessly placed in position. The excavated foundations of the earlier castles suggest that they were planned during the building process, without predetermined dimensions or design.

Influences from the Middle East and from Egypt can be recognized in the detail, but the modifications produced an individual style, clearly distinguishable from the vast scale of Egyptian work; and although almost every building which we know was produced in honour of the gods or for the use of the upper classes, the priesthood and the rulers, they appear, to our eyes and to our feelings, to be closer to human requirements. Correct scale seems to have become more important than sheer size.

In the early Aegean epochs the walls are still Cyclo-

pean, as if built by giants for giants; they stand uncouth before the beholder.

The buildings which arose in the islands were without prototype. There are no points of contact. Scanty influences from the East are only seen later, and then only in the ornamentation – not in the conception or ground-plan. Archaeology calls the style which arose in Crete and in the Aegean 'archaic', also 'Minoan' after Minos the legendary king, son of Zeus and the Phoenician princess, Europa, whom the god in the form of a bull had abducted.

According to legend Minos ruled over many islands, and to confirm his authority, the sea-god Poseidon made a bull rise from the waves, which Minos was to sacrifice. But the king decided to keep the beautiful animal and sacrificed a bull from his own herd. As a punishment for this deceit, Poseidon inflamed the king's wife, Pasiphae, with a wild passion for the bull, and by her command, Daedalus constructed a hollow cow out of wood. The queen crawled into this and

19

The palace of Minos. The foundation walls
according to the excavations of Sir Arthur Evans

KNOSSOS

coupled with the bull. From this union the Minotaur, a cannibalistic monster with a bull's head on a human body, was born. It was for this creature that Daedalus had to build the labyrinth, a maze with a thousand corridors.

This Greek myth supposedly represents the revenge of Attica for many humiliations during the Cretan overlordship. Every nine years Athens was obliged to send seven youths and seven maidens to Crete as fodder for the Minotaur — until the hero Theseus came and slew the monster.

In Homer's *Iliad* the island of Crete is portrayed as rich, powerful and adorned by a hundred cities. Heinrich Schliemann believed from childhood that Homer's epic was completely true and used it as his main guide during his search, in the second half of the nineteenth century, for evidence of ancient cultures. In 1870 Schliemann began his excavation of Mount Hissarlik in Asia Minor. Together with his friend and successor Wilhelm Dorpfeld, he exposed several cities built in strata one above the other. He identified the second from the bottom as the original of the Trojan legends but later chose the third. There is still some doubt about these identifications.

A few years later Schliemann went to Greece to search near Argos for the castle of Agamemnon, the Greek adversary of the Trojan lords. He started with excavations at Mycenae and neighbouring Tiryns through which our knowledge of Greek history was extended by over 1,000 years. The stories which to Schliemann had been credible from the beginning were now confirmed by the successful excavations. The myths were history written by poets.

In 1886 Schliemann went to Crete to search for the palace of Minos. In an olive grove above an expanse of ruins he thought he had found it. But he could not come to terms with the owner of the plantation, and so was not granted the satisfaction of crowning his life's work by revealing the glories of Minos. Schliemann died in Naples in 1890.

In 1900 the English archaeologist Arthur Evans (1851–1941) began to excavate the city of Knossos. He had hoped to complete the work in one year, but twenty-five years later he was still digging after having uncovered a huge field of ruins. Besides Knossos in the north, on the south coast of Crete the foundation walls and remains of large settlements and splendid palaces were excavated, some of which had been built before the year 3000 B.C.

The early epochs in the Aegean are obscure. There are no historical records. Only the legends give a notion of the power of the rulers on the islands. Remains of wall-paintings in the palaces tell, in their bright colours, of court life, of gymnastic exercises with bulls, which seem to indicate a mixture of sport and worship.

At a first glance the ground-plan of the palace of Knossos is confusing, a labyrinth, quite without geometry. There are no axes, no orderly flights. The

20

Reconstruction of a hall in the palace of Minos

Cyclopean wall of the Mycenaean period

building seems to have been planned with no regard to ceremonial needs. It is a building of passages full of corners. There are only a few really large rooms; even the throne-room is no longer than an ordinary living-room. Very many rooms have light-shafts, but the long store-rooms in the western wing are dark.

The squat columns in the courtyards of the palace suggest posts rammed into the ground by giant fists, and the massive capitals seem to have been pressed flat by the weight of the ceiling. The walls of the royal chambers were painted: slim figures stride across fields of lilies, framed by bands of watery waves and

plant motifs, interspersed at intervals with interwoven patterns of the snake-like arms of cuttle-fish.

Around 1700 B.C. a catastrophe overtook Crete, possibly linked with the conquests of the Hyksos from Iran, but more probably seismic. There are no decipherable records on papyrus or stone about its downfall. Knossos was later rebuilt, but about 1400 B.C. it was again completely destroyed, burnt out and plundered.

It seems natural to connect the downfall of Crete with the so-called Doric migration. But nothing can be proved. The Doric people, who had crossed the main-

The Treasury of Atreus at Mycenae in section; a pointed cantilever-vault on a hillside

land from the north and come to the islands, might possibly have landed on Crete after the destruction of Knossos.

We are inclined to imagine the Dorians as a heroic people, great in conquest and successful in establishing a new order. Undoubtedly this new order arose with the Greek language which they brought with them to Crete and spread through the islands.

From clumsy, barbaric beginnings there arose a style: the first which, with its great beauty, was to inspire posterity for all future time. This style and its characteristic temple-building order we call Doric, after the people who created both and of whose origins and beginnings we know so little.

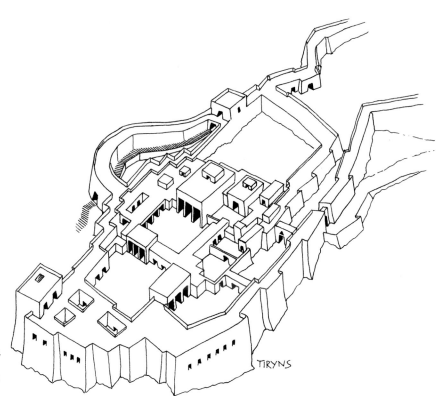

Reconstruction of the upper castle at Tiryns, begun apparently about 1400 B.C. The excavations were conducted by Schliemann and Dorpfeld

Classical Antiquity

Bronze head of Zeus from Olympia, *c.* 500 B.C.

Greece

The word 'classical' virtually signifies 'perfect'. We are accustomed to use the word in various connections. We recognize an epoch of classical music; we speak of the classical periods of great civilizations; of classical literature, architecture and even classical noses. In connection with 'antiquity', 'classical' indicates the flowering period of Greek art and Greek intellect.

This period did not begin immediately after the Doric migrations of 900 B.C. Some time was to pass before the new tribes merged with the indigenous inhabitants. The land and the islands were thinly populated when the Dorians came. The old inhabitants were apparently neither expelled nor exterminated, but the ruling class was new. From tentative beginnings a severe, statuesque style developed, to which many surviving stone sculptures bear witness: naked youths who can be identified as gods, or monuments from tombs, smiling tranquilly. And temples arose whose splendour can still be imagined, although no example has survived unimpaired by the ravages of time, earthquakes, wars or storms.

The model for the Greek temple was the *cella*, the square house with shallow saddle-roof. From the *cella* with a porch the temple was developed. The antae are the side boundaries of the porch, the extension of the side walls in the sense of the later column orders. In larger temples columns were erected between the antae, which helped to carry the pediment. Eventually the temple was surrounded on all four sides by rows of columns to provide a shaded walk. Although the whole building was executed in stone, the building principle nevertheless was based on the same principles as those of wooden buildings.

The Doric order in temple building has its greatest impact in the case of large free-standing buildings in elevated positions. The columns are squat in proportions, the relationship between thickness and height being often only 1:4. The forms are simple. The column stands sturdily on the ground, without a base; the shaft is ribbed, broadly chamfered, fluted. Such fluting presupposes skilled craftsmanship, for it is

23

more difficult to chisel out an exact groove than a channel with fillets. The massive shafts of the columns are slightly curved; this avoids a clumsy appearance in spite of their weight. The capital has no sculptured ornamentation. It is like a padded, compressed stone cushion (Echinus) under a square slab (Abacus). To our eyes the Doric column conveys a gravity, simple and very solemn. But when one considers that it was brightly painted in white, blue, red and gold, like the sculptured figures in the temple, then the words 'heavy' and 'solemn' are not relevant. The effect of a Doric building freshly painted was undoubtedly one of vigorous serenity.

In the sixth century B.C. on the Ionian islands and in the settlements on the Mediterranean coasts founded by the Ionians, new forms were developed — the columns of which were called 'Ionic' even at the time of their original diffusion. The Ionic style did not supersede the Doric: it represented a new style of

The Doric order: (left) corner of the pediment of a temple; (right) a Doric entablature. A = architrave, B = metope frieze, C = cornice
(facing page) Capital and entablature of the Ionic order; (right) ground-plans of Greek temples developed from the square house

decoration, for the sake of which the proportions but not the fundamental forms had to be changed.

Compared with the simplicity of the Doric, the ornamentation of the Ionic displays rich carving. Mouldings and cornices are adorned with patterns whose origins can be traced back to the early periods, gradually becoming more exact and more graceful. The entablature over the columns no longer has the Doric division into *metopes* but a continuous sculptured frieze. The columns are slender and the effect is lightened still more by the narrow fluting. They stand on a base, a pedestal, with an S-shaped profile. Typical of the Ionic capital is the thin *abacus* and below it, projecting sideways, the double scroll called a volute. This feature, which occurs now and again at

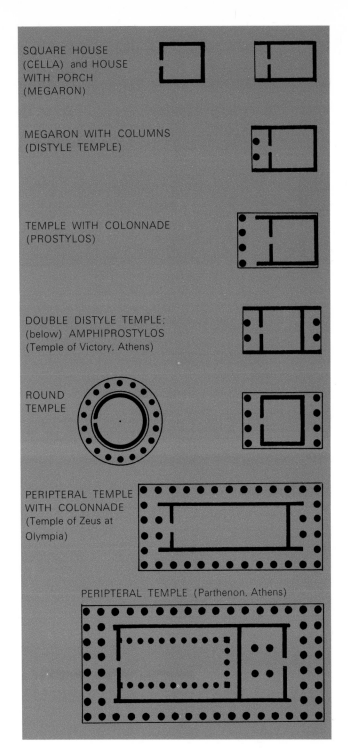

SQUARE HOUSE (CELLA) and HOUSE WITH PORCH (MEGARON)

MEGARON WITH COLUMNS (DISTYLE TEMPLE)

TEMPLE WITH COLONNADE (PROSTYLOS)

DOUBLE DISTYLE TEMPLE; (below) AMPHIPROSTYLOS (Temple of Victory, Athens)

ROUND TEMPLE

PERIPTERAL TEMPLE WITH COLONNADE (Temple of Zeus at Olympia)

PERIPTERAL TEMPLE (Parthenon, Athens)

Capital and entablature of the Corinthian order from the Hellenistic period

an earlier date, probably came from the East. One might describe the volute as a blanket rolled together from two sides to form a cushion like that which a porter lays on his shoulders to relieve the burden of the weight.

This idea corresponds to the effect which the capital has on the eye: the heavy entablature above it seems light. The Ionic order, as already stated, did not supplant the Doric. Both styles existed together. There are many temples whose exterior colonnades are Doric but whose interior columns are Ionic.

About 400 B.C. the third column-order arose in middle Greece and on the isthmus of Corinth, after which town the order is named. Its invention is ascribed to the sculptor Kallimachos of Attica. Its detailed and intensively carved decoration bears witness to the wealth of the period, to the desire for display and not least to the remarkable skill of the stonemasons. The Corinthian capital is characterized by the acanthus which has remained one of the commonest decorative motifs in architecture. The acanthus is a species of thistle with leaves that lend themselves well to stylization, either fanning out rather flatly or being more tightly rolled together according to the purpose or individual fancy of the artist.

The entablature and pediment of the Corinthian order are similar to the Ionic, at times perhaps somewhat overloaded, especially in buildings of the Roman period. The sparsely decorated early forms would not have suited this period so well, since the buildings of imperial Rome had always to embody ambition, might and wealth, not only through their size but rather through lavish refinement of detail.

In some Roman buildings the Corinthian capital underwent a modification. The so-called composite capital carries above the two acanthus garlands scroll-ornaments which are derived from the Ionic volutes.

The Corinthian decorative forms, even in their beginnings, point to an epoch which is moving away from the period which we call the 'antique' (in the narrow sense of the word) and towards a new direction which we call 'Hellenistic' in contrast to the Hellenic. By this we mean that the new and exuberant style has its roots in the Hellenic, that it develops and varies the old style. The earlier severe forms are submitted to a form of decoration which clothes the simple body of the building like a Sunday dress. The effect is richer, more costly, but no longer so noble. The style has not always been regarded thus. At certain periods, what we regard as Classical has been considered simple, almost impoverished. What our taste considers overloaded, was felt to be splendid and alone worthy to represent the importance of the epoch. This also applies to the important term 'Classicism' to be understood in the history of style as a tendency developing from the 'Classical' and transforming the fundamental forms in a new sense, often refining but sometimes weakening them. The term 'Classicism' is applied in the first instance to the Renaissance; and in the second instance to the period which succeeded the charming shell-ornamentation of the Rococo. But more of this later. For the present we must remain with the Romans, who enriched the wealth of forms inherited from the Greeks by two important principles: the circular building and the vault or arch.

The Greeks would have had no use for these forms. Arches and cupolas are entirely absent in their architecture. Round temples seldom occur — perhaps because the Greeks recognized that the round was not suited to their building principles. But two existing examples should be mentioned: the round Doric temple with a cone-shaped roof near the oracle at Delphi; and the Ionic Philippeion in the sacred grove of Olympia, which Alexander the Great had built in honour of his father Philip.

Only in building theatres did the Greeks give up their 'Classical' rectangle convincingly. In a horse-shoe shape, the steeply rising rows of seats for the spectators enclose the orchestra, either circular or semicircular, giving every seat a good view both of the chorus on the orchestra and of the actors on the stage.

In their theatre-building the Romans took over the Greek semicircle and later closed it to a full circle. Both forms — the open and the closed — have remained as models to this day. Even the old names have been retained: amphitheatre, arena, stadium, circus.

Capital in the colonnade of the Pantheon, Rome

The Acropolis at Athens

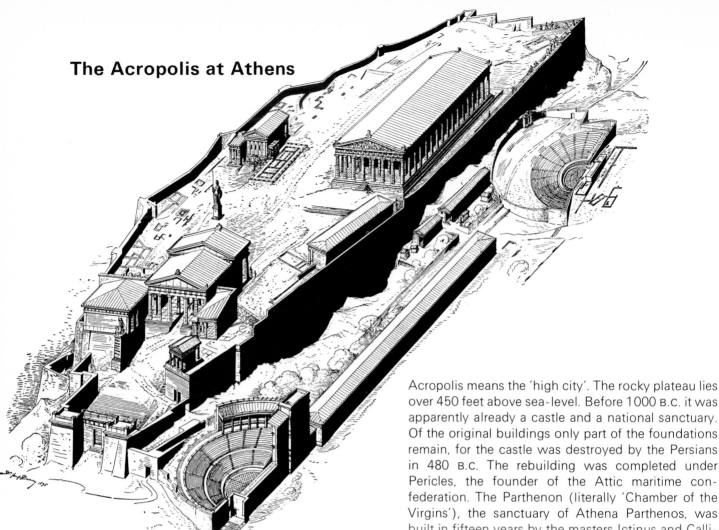

Drawing from Leo von Klenze's
attempted reconstruction

According to the Greek myths, Cecrops, who was endowed with the body of a snake, was the first king of Athens. His three daughters were given a sacred basket by Athene with strict instructions that they were always to keep it closed. Naturally they were overcome by curiosity and peeped inside — only to see Erechtheus, who also had a snake's body and a man's head. All three sisters were so terrified that they went mad and jumped to their deaths on the rocks below the castle.

Acropolis means the 'high city'. The rocky plateau lies over 450 feet above sea-level. Before 1000 B.C. it was apparently already a castle and a national sanctuary. Of the original buildings only part of the foundations remain, for the castle was destroyed by the Persians in 480 B.C. The rebuilding was completed under Pericles, the founder of the Attic maritime confederation. The Parthenon (literally 'Chamber of the Virgins'), the sanctuary of Athena Parthenos, was built in fifteen years by the masters Ictinus and Callicrates. The work was completed in the Doric style in the year 432. According to tradition the sculptures of Attic marble are by Phidias, the friend of Pericles.
On the eastern pediment the birth of Athena out of the head of Zeus was represented; on the western pediment the quarrel of the goddess with Poseidon over the land of Attica. The frieze is adorned with reliefs depicting combats between mortals and centaurs. Another frieze runs round the inner side of the entablature on which the pan-Athenian feast is represented. This feast was celebrated every four years. The carvings portray a procession in honour of the gods: men and women with sacrificial pitchers, sacrificial bulls, athletes in chariots and on horseback. There was only one road up the castle hill, on the east

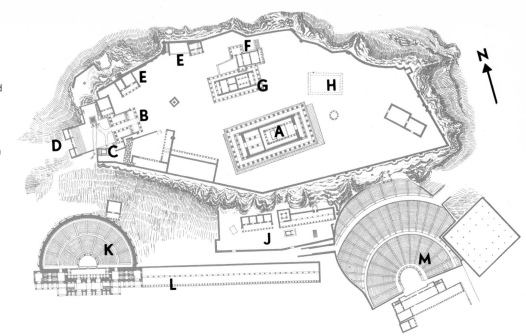

side. Here about the year 435 Mnesicles built a Doric entrance hall: the Propylaea. Beside this, on steeply falling rocks the delicate temple of the goddess of victory, an Ionic amphiprostyle, was erected about 420 B.C.

North of the Parthenon stands the Erechtheum, also built by Mnesicles about 410 in honour of Athena and of Erechtheus. This building deviates from the usual scheme of Greek temples. Only in the east does it have an Ionic vestibule in the usual sense. On its northern wall, lying somewhat lower, there is a hall. The south-west corner is adorned by the hall of Kore which can only be entered from within, a building whose entablature is borne not by columns but by six maidens facing south.

The Acropolis has suffered many vicissitudes. The Romans did not molest its shrines, and posterity has to thank them for copies of some sculptures which have long since disappeared. In the fourth century A.D. when Athena was 'expelled' by the Christians, the Parthenon became a church dedicated to the Virgin Mary. Reliefs with heathen representations were hewn off, and the statue of the goddess in gold and ivory was taken to Byzantium. After the Turks conquered Athens in the fifteenth century the Parthenon became a mosque and the Erechtheum

was converted into a harem. Later the Parthenon and the Propylaea were used as powder magazines. The Propylaea was struck by lightning which caused an explosion.

In 1687 the Parthenon was subjected to gun-fire by the Venetians; the roof collapsed and almost all the columns of one long side fell. The Venetians wanted to take the sculptures which had survived as war booty but most of them broke while they were being transported.

After the return of the Turks the English ambassador, Lord Elgin, obtained permission (in 1800) to ship the remaining sculptures and reliefs to London. The so-called Elgin Marbles are today exhibited in the British Museum.

From the stones of the Temple of Victory the Turks had built fortress walls. The German archaeologist, Ross, had the temple rebuilt as far as possible in 1835.

Ignorance coupled with lack of interest on the part of the Athenians allowed the Parthenon to become an impressive expanse of ruins. But today, aware of their heritage, the Greeks have ruled that not a single stone, not the smallest fraction of a statue, may be taken abroad, and archaeologists from all over the world co-operate in restoring and saving what can still be saved.

Reconstruction of an Etruscan temple, corresponding to the Greek temple with colonnaded façade. The space in front of the temple is U-shaped and surrounded by a wall. At the foot of the stairs stands the altar

Rome

Legend tells of two brothers, Romulus and Remus, who had been cast out. A she-wolf took them into her care and suckled them, and the shepherd Faustulus brought them up. According to the legend Romulus was the founder of Rome and its first king. His castle stood on the Palatine, one of the seven hills. The writer Varro (116–27 B.C.) ascribes the founding of the city to the year 753 B.C. in terms of our calendar, but there is no means of verifying this date. The dates of the early kings' reigns are equally not established. The names, Romulus and Remus, like the names of the succeeding kings — Numa, Tullus, Ancus, Tarquin — are of Etruscan origin. The Etruscans were a people of middle Italy who inhabited the regions between Tuscany and Latium. With the growth of Rome their name disappears from history. The Romans mastered Italy, spread their rule, conducted wars, traded and took possession of the Mediterranean ports which the Phoenicians and Greeks had founded. Six centuries later Rome had become the metropolis of the world, a city which continued to grow, until by the time of Julius Caesar it probably had over a million inhabitants and was the first large capital city in our sense of the word.

From the Etruscans they inherited the square house surrounded by a square wall (*Roma quadrata*). With willing admiration the Romans took over almost all the Greek forms of building and decoration, especially the Hellenistic. But more and more, as time went on the rows of columns were superseded by pillared arcades, and as if in acknowledgment of the Greeks, half-columns were finally placed before the pillars.

In the use of brick, in barrel-vaulting and cupolas the Romans gradually created their own style. In building technology they surpassed all the technical achievements of the Greeks. Artistically, however, they remained imitators and they created nothing to compare in majesty with the Acropolis at Athens.

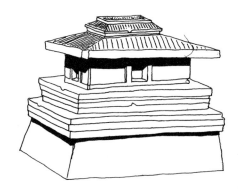

Clay model of an Etruscan house

But that is only our opinion; the Romans thought otherwise. This can be seen in the book, *De Architectura* by Vitruvius Pollio, written about 25 B.C. and dedicated to the Emperor Augustus. This volume, rediscovered in the fifteenth century, became the textbook for the architects of the Renaissance and the early Baroque. Vitruvius sees in the style which we call Hellenistic the culmination of architectural art. For us, looking back, this style is a beautiful dress suitable for Roman imperialism, but not always noble and often overloaded.

Architectural art in Greece was, in its great works, dedicated to the service of the gods. Even the theatres were consecrated places and not merely places of pleasure. We know little of Greek domestic building, but the simplest seems to have been good enough: a square space with the hearth in the middle, a small unadorned porch (megaron) seldom supported by columns, giving access to rooms without windows.

Roman architecture was faced with manifold problems. The State was its greatest patron, and with the growth of power developed the desire to display it. Even a purely utilitarian structure, such as an aqueduct, was considered worthy of an architectural presence, a façade.

The arch was the leading principle, applicable equally to a small aperture in a wall, and to victorious gateways like the triumphal arches erected to commemorate great political events. Temples, assembly halls, theatres, palaces, aqueducts and thermal baths — these were the commissions.

For the large assembly hall a new form evolved from the columned courtyard: the basilica. The word is derived from the Greek and denotes the official seat of the Archon basileus (King Archon) in the market-place at Athens. In Roman times, generally speaking every large hall was so designated: assembly hall, market hall or storehouse. Today the word is used only for churches, where the interior consists of three or five aisles, separated by columned arcades. The aisles are always lower than the central nave. The basilica may have a gable roof over wooden rafters; it may also be roofed by a barrel-vault. The columns carry the walls above a horizontal stone entablature or above an arcade. In basilica building ornamentation

Example of Roman pillar and arch construction, which was applied to many buildings, such as city gates, aqueducts and the Colosseum

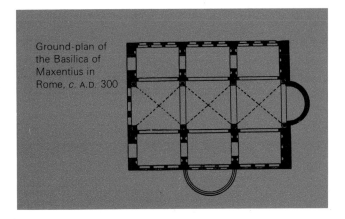

Ground-plan of the Basilica of Maxentius in Rome, *c.* A.D. 300

is confined to the interior and to the entrances at the narrow end. The basilica has remained one of the models for church building.

Less frequent but overwhelming in its effect of space is the Roman circular building spanned by one cupola or dome. The most distinguished example is the Pantheon, erected by the Emperor Hadrian to replace one built by Agrippa in the year A.D. 110, to honour Mars, Venus and the deified Caesar, which had been burnt down. The gigantic interior is lighted only by a circular opening in the cupola. The height of the cupola is some 120 feet, corresponding almost exactly to the diameter. Hardly another edifice of

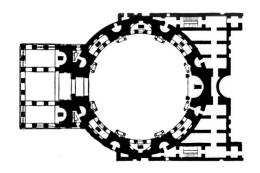

(facing page, top) Ground-plan of the
Pantheon. The walls on the right of the
Rotunda are part of the thermal baths

(facing page, bottom) Example of Roman
gate building: the aqueduct of the Emperor
Claudius, built c. A.D. 50. Today it is the
Porta Maggiore

(this page) The Pantheon: (top right)
frontal view; (below) longitudinal section
through the domed structure and vestibule

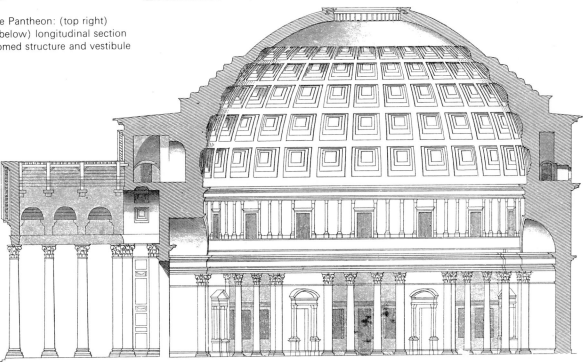

33

ancient Rome is so well preserved. It has been stripped of its exterior facing of marble and stucco, but the structurally significant brick masonry walls have, interestingly, become visible. In the course of time the interior of the Pantheon has suffered alterations in its decoration which are not always advantageous, but these have not lessened the monumental effect, which remains unforgettable.

Another less well-known example of the Roman round building is the fish market, built in the second century A.D., which was later dedicated as the church of S. Stefano Rotondo. The building is being restored, but as yet it has not been decided what will be done with the eighteenth-century wall-paintings.

In comparison to the Greek, we know a great deal about the Roman dwelling-house. It is an extension of the old Italic atrium-house. The atrium is the partly open interior, built in square form, the focal point of the house, from which all the surrounding rooms are accessible. In the middle of the atrium, exactly under the opening in the roof, a shallow basin called the *impluvium* is let into the ground. This was designed to catch the rain-water. Behind the house, and of the same width, there was often a small enclosed garden (*hortus*) or a peristyle, a square courtyard surrounded by columns.

It should not be supposed that all Romans lived in atrium-houses. Building sites would have been too expensive for this, especially in the imperial epoch. Poorer citizens lived in blocks of multiple dwellings, in many-storeyed terrace houses, and in flats that were nothing more or less than an endless ribbon-development of the old Etruscan hearth-house, usually without a porch or loggia.

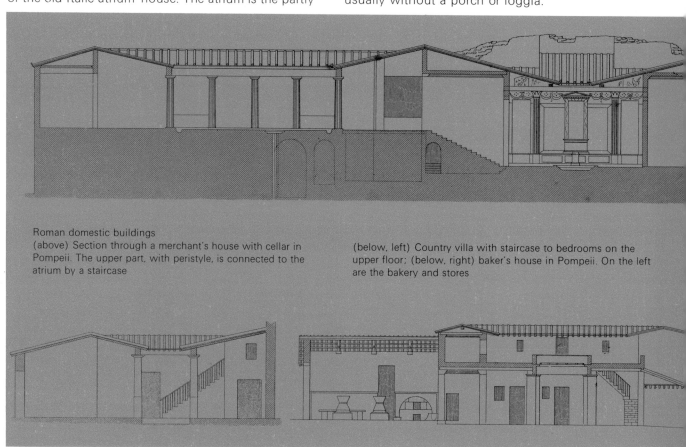

Roman domestic buildings
(above) Section through a merchant's house with cellar in Pompeii. The upper part, with peristyle, is connected to the atrium by a staircase

(below, left) Country villa with staircase to bedrooms on the upper floor; (below, right) baker's house in Pompeii. On the left are the bakery and stores

Roman composite capital from the Arch of Titus in Rome (*c.* A.D. 80); (right) triumphal arch of the Emperor Constantine, erected in Rome in A.D. 315 to commemorate victory over the usurper Maxentius. Free-standing columns are here placed in front of the pillars. The arch was surmounted by a quadriga with the triumphant emperor

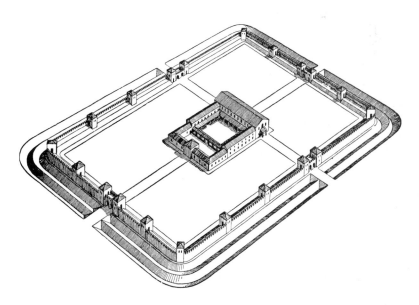

View of a Roman fort, planned in the traditional square and surrounded by ramparts and ditches. The roads divided the enclosure into quarters in which tents for the troops were erected. In the main building were the commandant's dwelling, drill halls and administrative offices. The fort became the nucleus of many Roman civilian foundations, and its layout can still be recognized in many town plans

35

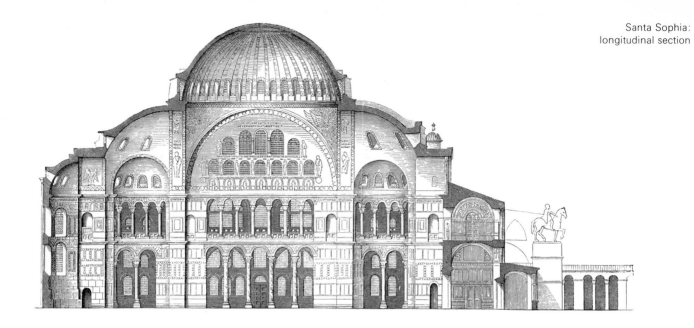

Diffusion and Transition

The world changes and this changes man's ways of thinking. Conversely, ways of thinking change and this changes the world. This applies especially to those turning-points in history when an old epoch is superseded. It also applies to the way in which past epochs are viewed. Formerly, pupils were tormented by innumerable figures and dates, and for the extinction of the West Roman empire the date 476 stood fast and became an important landmark. But Rome was not built in a day, neither was it extinguished in a day.

In A.D. 475 the young Romulus Augustulus was elevated to the throne by his father Patricius Orestes. But he was overthrown by the Germanic chieftain Odoacer; the father was slain, and the son pensioned off. Odoacer was recognized as king of Rome by Emperor Zenon (426–91), whose throne had long been by the Bosphorus.

Much had happened to prepare for this event. In the 122 years between the death of Marcus Aurelius A.D. 180, and the beginning of the reign of Constantine the Great (312–37) there had been a new emperor approximately every four years. In 330 the capital of the empire had been transferred to Byzantium, later known as Constantinople. The magical bond between the city of Rome and the throne had disappeared. The Roman empire could no longer be governed from Rome and the seat of government had been removed on military and political calculations.

Diocletian (284–305) built a residence for himself in Salona, now the Yugoslav town of Split, but this was to remain the seat of an emperor for less than a

During his lifetime the Emperor Justinian I set up two monuments
to himself: a comprehensive body of civil law, and Santa Sophia,
the church of Holy Wisdom. Building was begun in A.D. 532 by
the architects Anthemios of Tralles and Isidoros of Miletos. Five
years later the domes were vaulted. However, the chief dome
collapsed after a further twenty-five years, probably because of
earth movements, since the new dome, the shell of which was
only slightly thicker, has already stood firm for some 1,400 years.
The vault is a flattened arch, 126 feet in diameter and 236 feet
high at the summit. Although planned with a central focus, the
effect on the eye is that of a long hall. This is due to the two
half-domes which connect with the main columns to the east
and west. The interior was richly adorned with inlaid stonework
and mosaic. These pictures were thought to be lost when the
Turks transformed the church into a mosque, following their
conquest of Constantinople in 1453. The building itself suffered
little change: four minarets were added to the exterior; but all the
figures were plastered over and the surface was repainted. In
1837 the Swiss architect, Gaspare Fossati, was commissioned by
Sultan Abdul Necid to renovate the mosque. He first obtained
permission to uncover and sketch all the mosaics. This done he
had to hide them for the second time. Since 1932 Santa Sophia
has not been used as a mosque; Kemal Ataturk declared it a
Byzantine museum. It was then possible finally to expose the
mosaics

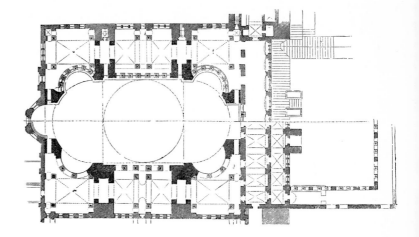

decade. After falling into disuse, the spacious courtyards were bricked up, arch by arch, and divided into
dwellings for the poor.

The architects of the time seemed to have few original
impulses. Moreover, it may be assumed that there
was a dearth of good craftsmen, a consequence of
the distress among the lower classes in the large
towns. The edifices and memorials of earlier emperors
became quarries for new buildings, which were then
decorated with the wall panellings, friezes, columns
and capitals of the older buildings. Sometimes this
new work showed a feeling for delicacy and proportion, but mostly it lacked artistry and understanding.
The few good architects available lived at or in the
proximity of the court, where they were fully
occupied in satisfying the ceremonial needs of the

court. The new Byzantine style was preceded by a
great deal of experimentation on established ground-
plans and by the appropriation of all manner of
details from buildings which no longer served any
useful purpose.

After the Christian religion was officially recognized
by the State, the Emperor Constantine ordered many
churches to be built, some of them quite large. None
of them have survived in their original form. But
following Constantine, and until the time of Justinian
(527–65), the early churches were erected full of
lovingly executed murals, rich in decoration and
joyously depicting the sacred stories.

The word 'Byzantine' suggests to us gold, silk and
splendour; the gigantic domes of Santa Sophia at
Constantinople; religious scenes and portraits of

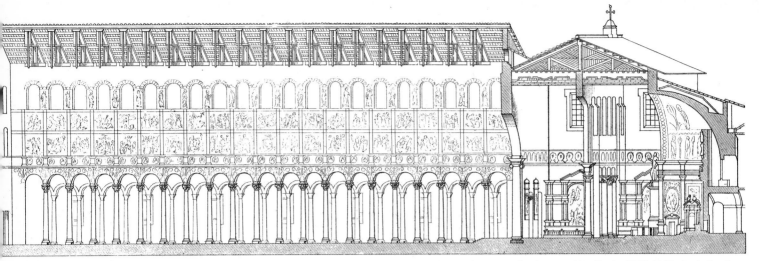

S. Paolo-outside-the-Walls, in Rome on the Ostia road. This church was founded by the Emperor Constantine over the grave of St Paul. In the ninth century it was plundered by the Saracens, and was almost totally destroyed by fire in 1823. With the help of donations from all over the world, it was rebuilt and consecrated by Pope Pius IX in 1854

Byzantine capital from Santa Sophia. Simple geometric transition from the circular column to the square support of the arch

Lombard font of the sixth century. Christian emblems and Nordic wicker pattern

emperors looking straight to the front. However, we should also think of the less monumental buildings, of the smaller churches which were erected wherever the new religion spread.

Besides the traditional basilica there arose a new ground-plan and with it a new building style for the church, the centrally planned building, which echoes the Roman circular building only in its dome. This building style underwent transformations in later centuries, but these changes were mainly restricted to decorative features and to other such variations which did not affect the basic principle. This principle may be expressed in a few words. The main and the lateral axes cross immediately under the centre of the dome and the building is co-ordinated around these axes. The dimensions of the nucleus of the building, that is the space covered by the dome, are of equal or almost equal length along both axes. The vaulting of the dome rests on walls, arches or columns which are related to each other quadrilaterally, hexagonally or octagonally. If the dome arises above a square base there is a transitional zone between the dome and its substructure from the square to the circular, which like the dome itself is already built in vaulted style. This zone is characterized by spandrels, which are also present when the substructure is hexagonal or

S. Paolo-outside-the-Walls. Four rows of twenty Corinthian columns support the arches of the five-aisled basilica

octagonal but are less noticeable because of their gentle curve.

The central space is capable of extension in all directions; for instance, through niches with semi-circular domes, lower than the main dome, or through square spaces surmounted by complete domes. In this way it is possible to enlarge the main space crosswise along the axes. Thus, transepts are created and longitudinally the building almost becomes a hall again.

The possibilities of variation and the freedom in the construction of the adjoining spaces were instrumental in giving the centrally focused building a new lease of life in the Baroque period.

39

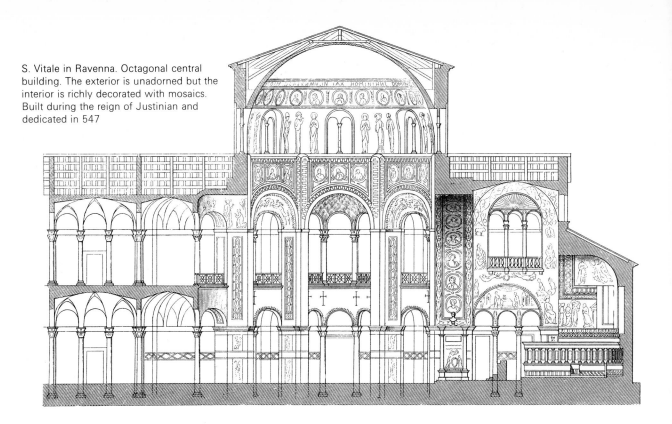

S. Vitale in Ravenna. Octagonal central building. The exterior is unadorned but the interior is richly decorated with mosaics. Built during the reign of Justinian and dedicated in 547

This style of building makes great technical and aesthetic demands. In measurement it requires great precision, and in construction it requires skilled and experienced masons, if it is to stand firm and to survive the centuries. It is therefore not surprising that it has nowhere been able to supplant the basilica. It may be noted that churches were often installed in ancient Roman buildings, especially in Italy, sometimes over the cellar of an earlier secret church dating from the time of the persecutions. In such cases the lower church became the crypt and was used for the burial of the devout.

Many of the Byzantine decorated churches are small, by no means masterpieces of the engineer's art, but their decoration, especially in mosaics and murals, is so attractive that they have been able to suffer the alterations of succeeding centuries without losing their pristine beauty. Their modest splendour is not intended to commemorate any one mortal, neither does it force an astonished 'Ah' or 'Oh' from the spectator, nor quicken the heart-beat like the Pantheon or Santa Sophia. Rather these small churches induce a reverent frame of mind in the believer, and for this they do not need to reflect the splendour of a vanished golden age. Indeed the early Middle Ages were not so golden despite the ostentation of the East Roman rulers.

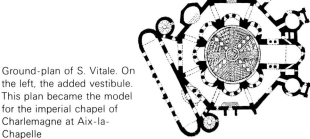

Ground-plan of S. Vitale. On the left, the added vestibule. This plan became the model for the imperial chapel of Charlemagne at Aix-la-Chapelle

40

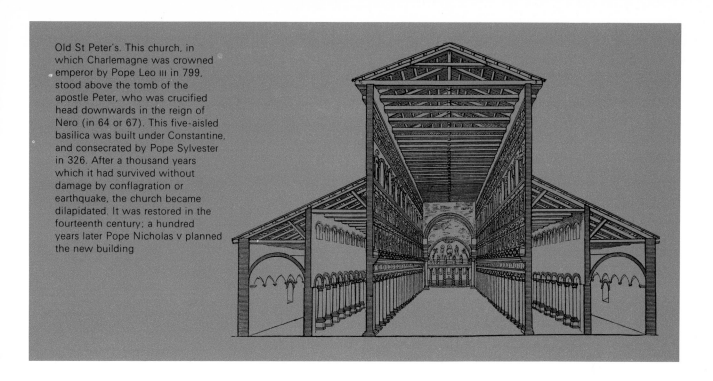

Old St Peter's. This church, in which Charlemagne was crowned emperor by Pope Leo III in 799, stood above the tomb of the apostle Peter, who was crucified head downwards in the reign of Nero (in 64 or 67). This five-aisled basilica was built under Constantine, and consecrated by Pope Sylvester in 326. After a thousand years which it had survived without damage by conflagration or earthquake, the church became dilapidated. It was restored in the fourteenth century; a hundred years later Pope Nicholas V planned the new building

Byzantine decoration depends upon Oriental motifs. But in the sixth century something was added which in its effect of snake-like tendrils seems to come not from the East but from the North.

From the middle Danube a Germanic tribe, the Lombards, had migrated into Italy; had occupied the district later named after them – Lombardy – and had penetrated as far as southern Italy. The new decorative forms which at first seem foreign to the Byzantine style may be ascribed to their influence. This is not to say that the Lombards had brought with them a new art or a new style. During their warlike incursions they would hardly have had the time to think of capitals and how to decorate them. But when they settled down, their uncouth individuality might well have found an outlet in new building forms. The forms of certain domestic roofs and wooden loggias can be ascribed to them. Many surviving metal locks and clasps bear the stamp of their work, as does a special kind of stone wall in which the rough construction (structure, stratification) is interrupted by continuous horizontal bands of small slanting (transverse) stonework.

The church of Saint Vitale at Ravenna, built 527–46, has above its delicate columns white marble capitals, whose interwoven filigreed scrolls have nothing at all in common with Ionic scrolls or with the old acanthus, neither do they bear any resemblance to Oriental arabesques. Rather do they remind us of northern patterns in wood-carving.

Although the Lombards became Christians they continually fought with Rome, and the Pope sought help from the Franks, who were gradually increasing their power over most of Europe. On Christmas Day in the year 800 Pope Leo III placed the crown on the head of the Frankish king (Charles), proclaiming him king of Rome. Soon afterwards the emperor in Constantinople acclaimed as his 'dear brother' the man whom the supreme pastor of Christendom had crowned.

The Franks had not come to Italy as immigrants like

the Lombards but as an army. They had no intention of settling in the South, and they returned home. Before Charles was crowned he had already been to Italy four times and had taken home new ideas in building, to lands across the Alps in which there were no stone buildings except those surviving from Roman times. During his reign, and after his death, there arose a new desire for learning in lands which had been laid waste by years of wars and migrations. Boundaries were established, and with the new security for life and property the soil was prepared for the cultivation of new ideas coming from the South.

In the various little States palaces were built, at first on the Roman model but then, gaining in originality, modified to suit the northern climate and the Frankish feeling for compactness and solidity.

The Byzantine gave way to the Carolingian, which was the forerunner of the later style that, in honour of its origins, came to be called the Romanesque.

Charles the Great, proclaimed by Wolfram von den Steinen 'Europe's Lighthouse', and claimed by the French as their own under the name of Charlemagne, brought back more with him than just ideas: books, relics, silk, the golden treasures of the Avars, classical pillars for his imperial chapel at Aix-la-Chapelle, for which he had bartered Saxon horses. He also imported the white elephant the Sultan Harun al Raschid had presented to him, but the animal soon died because the palace at Lippeham on the lower Rhine was too cold.

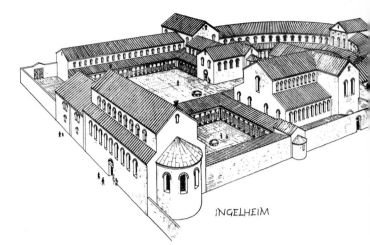

INGELHEIM

Reconstruction of the palace at Lippeham as an example of a Carolingian royal court with a royal hall (*aula regia*), arcaded courtyards, a basilica with transepts, and domestic buildings. This palace was destroyed by the French in 1689. The reconstruction has been drawn on the evidence of the surviving foundation walls

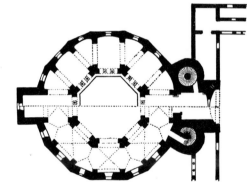

Ground-plan of the imperial chapel in Aachen (Aix-la-Chapelle). The lower half of the drawing shows the ground floor, the upper half shows the upper storey with the pairs of columns between the pillared arches

The imperial chapel of Charles the Great (Charlemagne) at Aachen (Aix-la-Chapelle), built by the royal architect Odo von Metz on the pattern of S. Vitale and completed in the year 805

(right) Longitudinal section; (below) diagrammatic drawing of the chapel and above this the silhouette of the minster as it is today, obscuring the old building to a great extent. On the left the lofty eastern chancel which was erected in the fourteenth century together with the octagonal dome. The bell tower over the porch is neo-Gothic

43

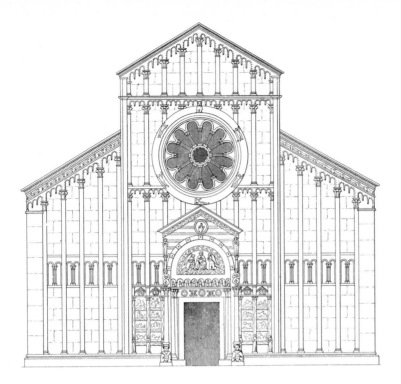

Romanesque

Charlemagne's great dream of combining central and southern Europe in one integrated kingdom did not survive his grandsons. The secular princes and the princes of the Church were not always the best of friends; and even when they were, it was a friendship more simulated than genuine. There existed a German empire which called itself holy and Roman, but little could be detected either of piety or of the antique Roman ideal of the State.

However, in considering the next few centuries, it is not necessary to harbour melancholy thoughts about the self-seeking, the hunger after power, or the spurious piety of the princes; for the epoch which we call 'Romanesque', constituted a stylistic unity, in spite of the quarrels of the princes. It produced the first real western European style. And as far as central Europe is concerned, it would seem as if all the builders and all the craftsmen had been pupils of one and the same master.

This was due to the monasteries, centres which had developed from settlements founded by missionaries since the fifth century. At first they were merely farming properties on land which had been cleared around the church. Soon, however, they came to be built according to an approved plan, of which the most significant examples are at Reichenau and St Gall.

The idea of the monastery was first realized in the East in conjunction with monks' cells. The word 'monastery' derives from the Greek word meaning 'alone'. It was a place of gathering for communal meditation undisturbed by the world, and a place for communal living.

As early as the year 530 Benedict of Nursia had laid down explicit rules for the monastic life when founding the monastery of Monte Cassino in central Italy: regular divine service, communal meals, communal dormitories. Charlemagne, and Louis the Pious

44

after him, accepted the Benedictine Rule as a model, and ordered the addition of monastery schools — the only schools which existed in the Middle Ages. All later monastic orders are derived from the original Benedictine conception.

From the unity of these widely diffused rules, the stylistic unity seems to follow. The Christian power was the superior, indeed the only, building patron, and in spite of the political confusion and of the bickerings about frontiers and privileges, this unity was maintained.

The word 'Romanesque' only came to be widely used in the nineteenth century. Previously various names had been given to the various periods, none of which seem particularly suitable. 'Byzantine' was used as long as there was some obvious connection with Constantinople. Sometimes the style was called 'neo-Greek', which was just as false as 'old-German'. For the style was neither Greek nor German nor Roman, nor could it truthfully be named after any particular region. It was simply European.

The word 'Romanesque' is a good one, for it recalls the origin of the stylistic features: the basilica, the Roman round arch, the arcaded courtyard. The Romanesque style may be applied to all buildings which were erected between the end of the tenth century and the thirteenth although this statement must be modified by noting that as early as the twelfth century new building principles were being

The flight out of Egypt. Example of a Romanesque capital with representations of men and animals. From St-Andoche, Saulieu

devised in France and England which led to the Gothic style.

In its beginnings the Romanesque continued to use and develop the Carolingian vernacular. The thirty years preceding and following the year 1000 are often referred to in Germany as the Ottonian-Saxon early Romanesque. The limits of this epoch are sometimes given as the years 936 and 1024, being respectively the dates of Otto I's coronation and the death of the Emperor Henry II, founder of the bishopric of Bamberg. As with all styles, however, exact dates are too arbitrary.

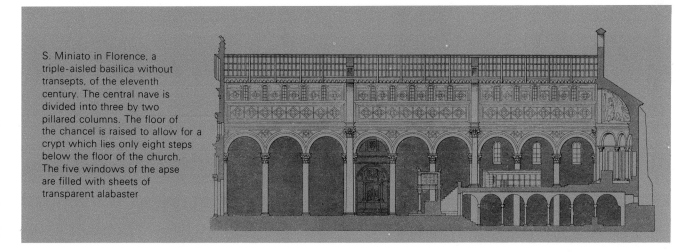

S. Miniato in Florence, a triple-aisled basilica without transepts, of the eleventh century. The central nave is divided into three by two pillared columns. The floor of the chancel is raised to allow for a crypt which lies only eight steps below the floor of the church. The five windows of the apse are filled with sheets of transparent alabaster

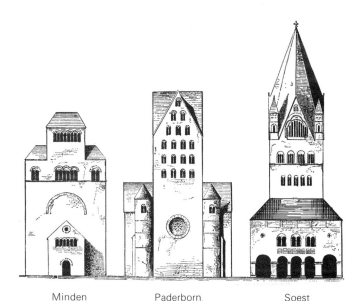

Three examples of Romanesque façades

Minden   Paderborn   Soest

The works of the Romanesque period are predominantly ecclesiastical, and the old building ideas were enriched in every way. Through the accentuation of the western façade the basilica received a new face. Towers now flank the western entrance, often extending beyond the breadth of the building, and the so-called west front is created. These towers are often named after the archangels Michael and Gabriel, which seems to suggest echoes of heathen beliefs, for out of the western sunset the demons of darkness were supposed to come. The west front was considered a bulwark against such evil spirits, all the stronger for being dedicated to the archangel who bears a sword for slaying dragons. The second important difference from the old basilica is the increased emphasis on the crossing, the space which the nave shares with the transepts as they cross it at right angles. Because of this space the nave is extended eastwards. Thus arises the choir which forms a single spatial unit with the apse, now widened to the width of the nave. The floor of the choir is always elevated

Worms cathedral. This sketch shows the building without the chapels and sacristies which were added later. The church was built over former foundations towards the end of the twelfth century. It has a chancel at each end. The western chancel (right) was completed in 1230. As well as the four round towers there were octagonal domes with ribbed vaulting under tent-roofs above the crossing of nave and transepts and above the western chancel

above the floor-level of the main building, even if only by a few steps. Usually there is access from the choir to the crypt, which derives its name (Greek: 'hidden') from the early Christian subterranean tombs of the martyrs. Characteristic of German Romanesque is the double-chancelled church (e.g. Mainz, Worms) which has a choir at each end of the nave.

Barrel-vaults and domes are seldom found in early Romanesque. The nave is surmounted by a ceiling which is secured to the rafters of the saddle-roof. But after 1100 nave and transepts are covered by barrel-vaults which meet to form a cross. Besides this cruciform vault there is a second method of closing the space above the nave and transepts. The vault of the nave ends at the cross-beams of the crossing. The crossing itself, in this case carried up higher, is vaulted separately, either with a barrel or a dome, from which the later cross-ribbed vault evolved. The vaulting above the crossing can only be suspected from outside the church, as it is usually surmounted by a tent-roof, corresponding to the saddleback roofs of nave, transepts and west front.

In the decorative forms of Romanesque buildings, although not in the sculptured figures, influences of ancient ornamentation are often to be seen. Oriental and Byzantine ornament are also borrowed and adapted. In western Europe these are supplemented by new Nordic elements, which might have been brought in by the roving Normans.

The Romanesque ecclesiastical style must undoubtedly have influenced the secular buildings of the period. But unfortunately very few such buildings have survived the centuries undamaged, since they were either destroyed by fire or they collapsed, and remain as venerable ruins. Others were constantly being reconstructed and suffered extensive alteration in later years.

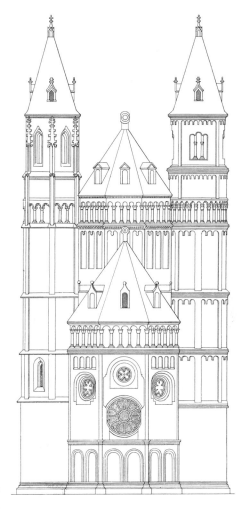

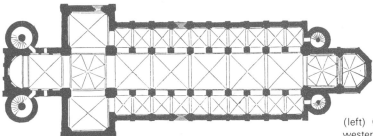

(left) Ground-plan of Worms cathedral; (right) elevation of the western chancel with dwarf gallery and blind arcade decoration

47

Notre-Dame la Grande in Poitiers. The drawing shows the remarkable façade of the church, distinguished by the richness of the sculptured figures in the two-storeyed arcades; an unusual feature of façade design in the Romanesque period. The clustered columns and the lofty window over the central door already anticipate Gothic forms. Above the large central window a mandorla, also called an 'almond-halo'. This motif, which represents the Madonna surrounded by an almond-shaped halo, is adapted from the technique of the mediaeval illuminated manuscript

St Mark's in Venice. In the year 829
Venetian seafarers brought the
bones of Saint Mark to Venice
from Alexandria. One year later
work was begun on a church to
house the relics of the patron saint
of the city. This church was
destroyed in the great fire of 976

In the eleventh century the
Venetians built the new cathedral
after Byzantine and Oriental models
with five lofty domes which likewise
are surmounted by Oriental onion-
shaped lanterns. The whole
building has — inside and out —
almost 500 columns. It also houses
the treasure chamber of this
powerful trading city. In the
fifteenth century the façade was
decorated with Gothic pinnacles
and with an ogee arch over the
main entrance. The antique gilt-
bronze horses on the balcony were
booty from Constantinople

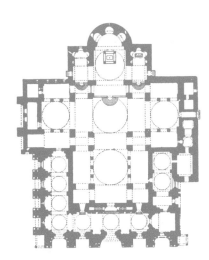

49

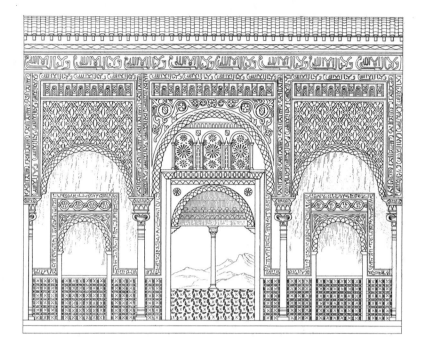

Arcades and wall patterns in the Myrtle Court of the Alhambra ('Red castle'), the castle of the Moorish kings in Granada, from the thirteenth century

The Islamic Style in Spain

In the seventh century the Arabs began to swarm out of their desert lands and to spread far and wide to the south and to the north, for the prophet Mohammed had commanded them to conquer the world. They destroyed the Persian kingdom of the Sassanidae and they wrested the provinces of Syria and Palestine from the East Roman Empire. In the year 641 they conquered Egypt and founded the city of Cairo. Seventy years later their general, Tarik, occupied the isthmus between the Iberian mainland and the stretch of country which was later named after him: Mount Djebel-al-Tarik (Gibraltar); in a seven-day battle on the Guadalete he destroyed the kingdom of the Visigoth Roderic. In 756 the Umayyad Abd-ar-Rahman founded the Emirate of Cordoba.

The Arabs were masters of Spain for over 700 years, but at no time did their influence on building styles extend over the whole of the peninsula. Generally speaking their power did not extend beyond the Tagus, on which Toledo lies. The most northerly Arab city was Calatayud, home of the famous golden ceramics of Toledo.

Once, in the year 731, an Arab army had penetrated as far as Tours and Poitiers, but they were repulsed by Charles Martel.

The Arab word *Islam* signifies 'Submission to the Will of God' and this is intrinsic to Islamic culture, which arose solely from its religious context and was then embraced by many peoples; Iranians, Turks, Syrians, Kurds, Egyptians, Berbers and others.

Islamic intellectual achievements in philosophy, science and mathematics have had a permanent influence on European thought, but Islamic architecture was limited solely to those regions which actually belonged to the Arabs, such as the southern half of Spain and the Balearics.

The technology of building, the use of brick, and the art of vaulting came from the East. Ornamentation is a modification of motifs derived from the whole of Asia Minor. A considerable enrichment of ornamentation ensued through the inclusion of Arab written characters, endlessly repeating the monograms of Allah and of the Prophet in decorative series or filling flat spaces. The use of written characters as an ornamental motif, often so elaborately interwoven as to be no longer legible, has the task of replacing that which the Prophet decreed should not be represented: firstly the Godhead in human form and secondly any human form whatsoever. In the Islamic world, in so far as it obeys the *sunna* (or tradition) the human image may not be portrayed. For the Shiites (i.e. the separated Ones), who also do not undertake the pilgrimage to Mecca, the *sunna* is not binding; and it is to this fact that the world has to thank the Persians for the magical world of their miniatures.

In the organization of space the Islamic architects learned much from Byzantium. The Christian church of Santa Sophia was the model for many later mosques. The outer court surrounded by colonnades, and containing a fountain, that leads into the mosque corresponds to the Christian monastic courtyard, architecturally if not in religious significance. But specifically Islamic is the minaret (from the Arabian word *manara* meaning lighthouse). From here the muezzin calls the faithful to prayer five times a day.

In Islamic architecture every possible kind of arch is used. To begin with the Arabic architects seemed to favour the round arch and the capital, designed together as one unit. Thus the hoof-shaped arch came about. Then they felt the desire to make the height of the arch independent of its span; so they produced the steep and the broad pointed arch. The Arabic pointed arch does not always consist of continuous curves. Often the two halves start curved, then become straight until they meet in the middle in a more or less pointed fashion. The so-called ogee arch, a form found frequently in late Gothic, seldom occurs. Aesthetically pleasing, and of frequent occurrence, is the clover-leaf arch; this is also found in late Romanesque buildings, but the Arabs

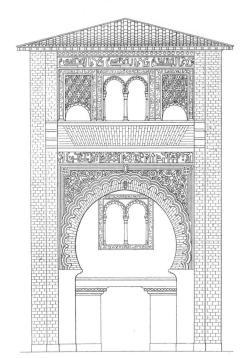

Hoof-shaped arch on the façade of a private house in Granada

Clover-leaf arch remodelled as a double superimposed fan-arch from the great mosque at Cordoba. This building, begun in the eighth century, was enlarged and newly decorated in the tenth century

51

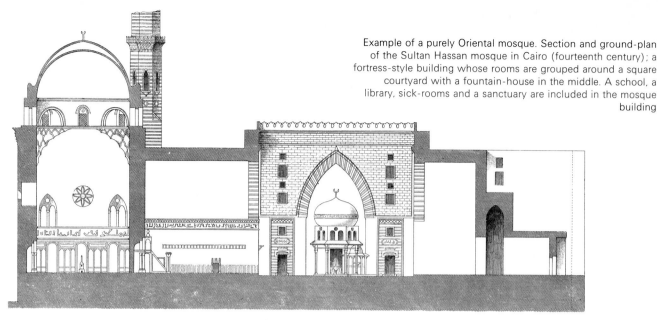

Example of a purely Oriental mosque. Section and ground-plan of the Sultan Hassan mosque in Cairo (fourteenth century); a fortress-style building whose rooms are grouped around a square courtyard with a fountain-house in the middle. A school, a library, sick-rooms and a sanctuary are included in the mosque building

modified it further to form the fan arch. This is purely decorative and is found in many variations, although its transverse strength is only slight, so that it has to be surmounted by a round arch to sustain the weight of the ceiling. Fan arches adorn the great mosque at Cordoba where, like a bracelet between the slender columns, they give a strangely airy feeling to the space.

All the architectural and decorative features designed for the mosque in praise of Allah are found again, modified and reduced in scale, in the secular buildings. In addition we find elaborately carved trellis-work in wood on doors and windows, stucco-work and ceramic wall- and floor-tiles whose decorative designs ingeniously span whole stretches of tile-work, which is correlated with the wall treatment as a whole.

In 1492 the rule of Islam in Spain came to an end. Ferdinand and Isabella, the 'Catholic Kings', captured Granada for Spain and for Christendom. Boabdil-Abdallah, the last Arab ruler, was forced to withdraw to Africa.

The principles of Islamic architecture did not survive in Europe, except sporadically when architecturally minded princes in search of exotic originality imitated Arab forms. Islamic ornamentation, on the other hand, has persisted: in ceramic design, in silk-weaving, in printed fabrics, in carved ornaments. And finally there is one word which we have perpetuated to denote many variations of interlaced ornament and playful intricacy, delicate, charming, meaningless but beautiful: Arabesque.

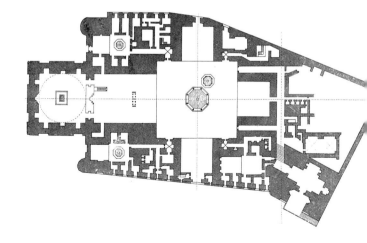

Drawings from the architectural sketch-book of Villard de Honne-court, probably about 1240. The book contains more than 300 pen-and-ink drawings on parchment: building details, machines, construction plans, with explanations not always capable of interpretation. It also contains representations of the human figure such as the disciple on the Mount of Olives

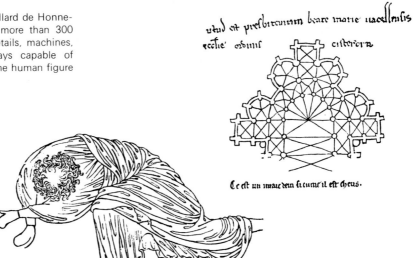

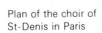

Gothic

Saint Denis (Latin: Sanctus Dionysius), whose feast day is celebrated on the ninth of October, is one of the national saints of France. He died a martyr's death in the third century and is counted among the fourteen Helpers in Need.

In the year 1144 the Abbot Suger dedicated a church to Saint Denis. Its choir had taken five years to build. The abbot wrote a book about the construction of this church, which contains the following passage:

'The nave is supported by twelve columns, corresponding to the twelve apostles, with just as many in the aisles, corresponding to the twelve prophets. Thus are fulfilled the words of the apostle who built in the spirit: So you are no longer guests and strangers, but fellow-citizens with the saints and members of God's house, which is built upon the foundation of the apostles and the prophets, with Jesus as the corner-stone unifying both walls, and in which every building, be it spiritual or material, grows to become a holy temple in the Lord.'

The abbot's book gives many other pointers to symbolical references: numbers become significant, intentions are named and given reasons. All kinds of technical problems, and difficulties encountered during the building, as well as solutions in achieving the envisaged plan: all are expounded in long Latin sentences. But one thing is missing: the name of the architect. It is plain from the text that the abbot himself was not the architect.

It sounds strange to say that the unknown creator of the church of St-Denis was the discoverer of the Gothic; yet this is almost the truth. For this unknown master had created a new method of building; he had pondered over the power of stones to resist stress; he had reduced walls to columns with intervening spaces so as to allow the light to stream through the windows into the church — windows which were as large as the height of the choir allowed. The lower storey of the choir of the church of St-Denis has survived, enough at least to let us see the significance of the building. The stature of this master-builder is by no means diminished by saying that he did not discover the chief elements of the Gothic style: the pointed arch and the buttress; and that the ground-

Plan of the choir of
St-Denis in Paris

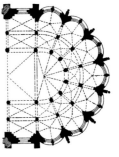

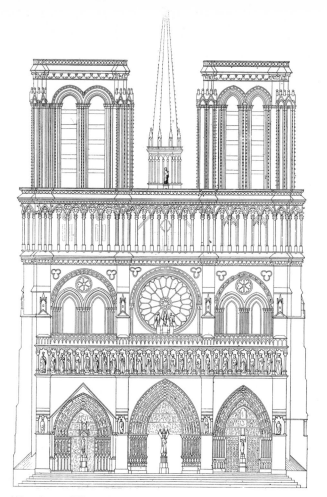

West front of Notre-Dame in Paris. The building was begun by Bishop Maurice de Sully soon after his assumption of office in 1160. Choir, nave and west front were completed in 1225; portal façades of the transepts in 1270

plan is nothing more than a five-aisled space, with the side aisles forming a semicircle around the choir.

The first pointed arch of which we know — looking like a Gothic arch, although somewhat plumper — adorns a building on the island of Rhoda in the Nile near Cairo, which served to measure the water-level. It dates from the beginning of the seventh century.

The Romans used buttresses to neutralize the outward pressure of vaults, and it should be noted that ribbed vaulting was also not new in the twelfth century. But the choir of St-Denis represents a new system in its unity of technical and aesthetic innovations which are inextricably linked. In the Gothic it is not the technical aspect alone which is important, which is new, which is sublime. Rather it is the technical advance which has made possible the new use of space, the new vision of form. No longer need these elements conform to a monotonous series of equal vaults as was inevitable with the round-arched barrel-vaults. Pillars no longer have to stand four-square; pointed cross-vaults maintain their stability over a rectangle and the height of the pointed arches can remain the same even when the spans are varied.

Finally, the delicate tracery which we regard as typically Gothic is something which the system evolved, an ornamentational repetition of the constructional principles in the decoration, a manifold echo repeating the main forms. What proved to be necessary in the structure as underpinning, climbs over the tracery, over the buttresses, over decorated gable-ends and pinnacles and dances along the

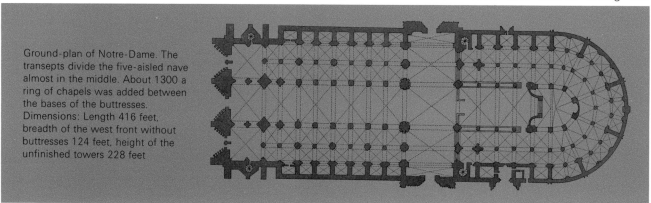

Ground-plan of Notre-Dame. The transepts divide the five-aisled nave almost in the middle. About 1300 a ring of chapels was added between the bases of the buttresses. Dimensions: Length 416 feet, breadth of the west front without buttresses 124 feet, height of the unfinished towers 228 feet

edges of the filigree towers straight into the clouds: a chorale in stone glorifying the devout zeal of a master-builder and his associates. The great counterpoint to everything striving upwards crowns the west front in gigantic splendour: the rose window, symbolizing the sun, the stars, the world, offering a thousandfold possibilities of fresh designs. The sum total of the Gothic is very much more than mere technical skill and geometry.

It is difficult for us today to understand why the Gothic, in its origins a regional matter of the 'Cathedral-landscape', for instance, at first found no recognition in Italy. It appeared there very much later in the fourteenth century and was only granted a short lease of life, hardly more than a hundred years, only to give way to the Renaissance of the antique in the zeal of the new humanism.

The word 'Gothic', which for us today is charged with an almost excessive emotional content, was first used in Italy during the Renaissance period and was intended to be an expression of contempt. Giorgio Vasari (1511–74), painter, architect and art authority, used the word *gotico* when he wished to represent something as being barbaric, without roots in the antique. The word retained the interpretation which Vasari had intended until the eighteenth century as a designation for something intricate and overloaded, for a building without taste. Starting in the Romantic period the word became charged with the significance which it has for us today.

To Goethe recognition came earlier. When he went to Strasbourg he expected to see the cathedral — in his own words — as a mis-shapen, bristling monster. But in his essay: 'On German architecture' which he wrote in 1772 he described his impression of Strasbourg, finishing with the words: 'It is good.'

Then, in the middle of the nineteenth century, reports were discovered from the time of the cathedral building and these were translated and published. Through these, admirers came to obtain a picture of the conditions under which the cathedrals grew.

Robert de Mont-St-Michel wrote in 1194:

'In this year we saw for the first time the faithful harnessing themselves to carts which were loaded with stone, wood, corn and other materials which were necessary for the work of building the

A contrast: on the left a Gothic basilica. The aisles are considerably lower than the nave, the roof is lowered. The buttressing, pillars and half-arches are visible. On the right a Gothic hall-church. Nave and aisles are of equal height and are covered by a single saddle-roof. The buttresses are built up without arches. Both systems are here shown in cross-section. The sectional planes are in black

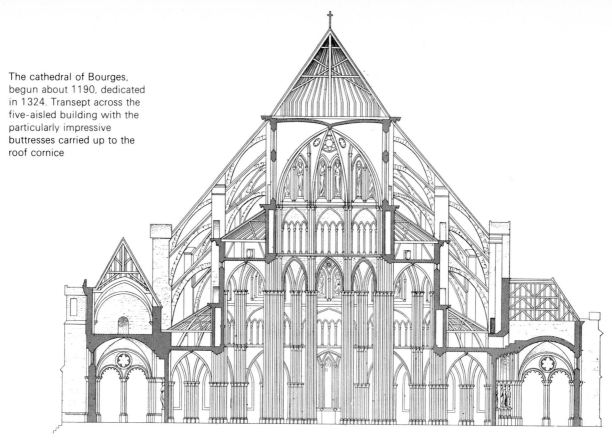

The cathedral of Bourges, begun about 1190, dedicated in 1324. Transept across the five-aisled building with the particularly impressive buttresses carried up to the roof cornice

cathedral. As if by magic the towers rose up. And this was happening not only here but everywhere in France, in Normandy and in other regions. Everywhere men humble themselves, everywhere they do penance, everywhere they forgive their enemies. One saw men and women dragging heavy loads through marshland and praising God in song for the wonders they saw rising up before their eyes.'

A few years later Abbot Hailmon of St-Pierre-sur-Dive wrote:

'When before has the like been seen or heard, that powerful rulers and princes of this world, inflated with riches and honours, that even women of noble birth have bent their proud heads, have yoked themselves to carts like beasts of burden, in order to bring wine, oil, corn, lime, stone, wood to the men building a church? And although there might be more than a thousand people gathered together, silence prevails, no word is heard, not even a whisper. When they pass by to the sound of trumpets and with consecrated banners flying, nothing can stop them, neither mountains nor rivers. You might believe you were witnessing the ancient Hebrews passing over the Jordan. The Lord God seems to be leading them in person. The waters of the sea have parted to give them passage. Witnesses at St-Marie-du-Port have affirmed all this. When the pilgrims have arrived at the church, in the building of which they are assisting, they build a castle with their carts and keep watch all through the night singing psalms. Candles and lamps are lit on each cart, relics are brought to the sick who have accompanied the procession, and intercession and prayers are offered for their healing.'

The names of many of the early Gothic master-builders are unknown. The Abbot Suger of St-Denis did not name his architect. But this was not because of any malicious intention; the names did not matter.
But later, this was not so. The fame of these masters

spread beyond the place in which they worked, their names passing from mouth to mouth. They were called to work on buildings which had long been neglected, and they were well paid for their work.

At Canterbury the monks were building the nave of their future cathedral, when in the year 1174, the choir was destroyed by fire. The monks were despondent, for they could not decide whether it would be better to demolish the remaining building or to risk adding to it. They brought in William of Sens from France, who directed the building of the choir for five years. The monk Gervase writes as follows:

'. . . but at first he concealed from us what he thought to be inevitable, for he feared that the full truth would overwhelm us in our hopelessness. In the meantime and with the help of others he made his preparations, and when he felt that the monks were beginning to overcome their feeling of despair he admitted that the damaged columns and everything which they supported would have to be pulled down if the monks laid value on the safety and perfection of their church. William had stone brought in from abroad. He invented the most astonishing machines for the loading and unloading of the ships and for the transport of the stone. In addition he gave the stonemasons wooden models for their chiselwork.'

In the fifth year of his work at Canterbury William of Sens fell from the scaffolding. After this he could no longer walk or stand, and he deputed the conduct of the building to a skilful monk who had been his foreman. From his bed he gave instructions. But as the doctors held out no hope of recovery he finally returned to France in order to die in his homeland.

In 1235 the French architect, Villard de Honnecourt, wrote an illustrated book for his pupils, and one of the things we have learnt from it is that the Gothic method of building did not involve the use of an accurate scale. A basic measure was adopted, and by means of multiplication and division of this measure the measurements for the whole and for individual parts were arrived at. A great deal of drawing was done, but little calculation. Scholars are agreed that the builders hardly had an adequate knowledge of

structural stability. What they had was a feeling for dimensions, for the strength of walls and the thickness of columns, for the burdens which different kinds of stone would bear. It was all geometry developed from a few fundamental shapes: the square, the half-square, the circle and the arc. Compasses and the plumb-line were important. Of calculation they understood little, but with this little they were able to give the world something which was more than worldly. And it was this for which some pert humanists coined the word 'Gothic'.

Modest as they were to the point of intentional anonymity, these master-builders were nevertheless sufficiently conscious of their achievements to earn the praise with which Solomon extols the Creator: By measure and number and weight thou didst order all things.

The embellished gable above the Gothic window of Ste-Chapelle, Paris, 1248

The Marienburg on the Nogat in East Prussia, founded in 1272, and after 1309 seat of the Grand Master of the Teutonic knights who had until then lived in Venice. The Grand Master's palace here illustrated was finished in 1360. In 1410 Henry of Plauen defended the castle successfully against the Poles. A second attack forty years later was also repulsed. But in 1457 the castle was sold to Poland by the mercenaries of the order

After the first division of Poland the Marienburg passed into the possession of Prussia and was used as a barracks. The Grand Master's palace became a corn depot and gradually fell into decay.
In 1799 the architect Friedrich Gilly published an illustrated book drawing attention to the great cultural and artistic value of the castle. Consequently a comprehensive plan of restoration was carried out in the nineteenth century and completed in 1914.
Today the Marienburg is again in the possession of Poland. Since 1950 the Polish Department of Public Monuments has been working on the restoration following the damage of the Second World War

What drove the men who built these lofty houses for God, in such new forms, and rising so high above the roofs of the crooked and crowded towns? Was Christendom in danger, so that it was necessary to present visually to doubting minds something which they could not pass by? Christendom was not in danger in this sense, but the church which Helena, the mother of Constantine the Great, had caused to be built over the holy tomb in Jerusalem, was. Since the Islamic Fatimides followed by the Turks had been masters of Palestine, pilgrims no longer had undisturbed access to their goal.

In 1095 Pope Urban II had proclaimed the First Crusade. Geoffrey of Bouillon with six other princes had marched to the East. By various routes they had led 200,000 soldiers to Constantinople. Often stretched to the point of exhaustion, the host of crusaders had destroyed the Islamic strongholds in Syria, stormed Jerusalem and after a terrible bloodbath had completed their pilgrimage to the church of the Holy Sepulchre.

But this hard-won victory was short-lived. Although the popes of the twelfth and thirteenth centuries summoned the princes of Europe time after time, although strong and well-led armies marched to the East and fought, yet the holy places remained ultimately in the hands of Islam.

Fighters great and small had been moved to answer the call out of religious dedication, out of ascetic motives or merely out of a desire for adventure. Many perished. But in spite of all the misery and the loss of human life, the consequences of the Crusades were

in many respects significant for Europe: cities flourished through the impetus to trade over land and sea; in philosophy and science knowledge was stimulated by contacts with the Arabs; new monastic orders were founded: Carthusians, Cistercians, Premonstratensians, Dominicans, Franciscans, Carmelites and Augustines. Of equal importance was the later development of the religious knightly orders, which had been founded during the Crusades: the Templars, the Knights of St John and the Teutonic Knights. With the orders, both monastic and chivalrous, came the Gothic builders, and from southern France to the Baltic lands, Gothic is the universal style of the later Middle Ages, but each land produced its own version. This may be due to varying temperaments, to the availability of building materials,

and not least to different local problems, which were no longer merely clerical and monastic, as at the time of the Gothic beginnings in France, but now embraced the growth of the cities and trade. Castles and citizens' houses, palaces, town halls, cloth halls and storehouses all speak one architectural language and employ one principle: the thin wall between pillars, the pointed arch, tracery on windows and gables.

The development of the Gothic in France probably shows the greatest continuity. The culmination is the period around 1250, but it would be a mistake to regard the following years as a period of decline. During their building period, often very long, the great cathedrals were subjected to changes from the original plan. No doubt the impetus of the earlier age

59

often weakened. We see evidence of this in many half-finished towers. According to the original plan Chartres, for instance, should have had nine towers; only two were built, dissimilar, and one of these looks as if it were borrowed. For other projects seven towers were no rarity: two over the west front, two at the end of each transept, and the largest over the crossing. Many of these towers were left unfinished, not because of financial difficulties nor because of a shortage of craftsmen, but if was often thought advisable not to add to the burden on the foundations. So ideal cathedrals, as Viollet-le-Duc sketched them, were never built, and the many-towered prototype gave way to the cathedral with two main towers, although the west front with only one tower over the main portal is also a convincing solution. In contrast to the Italian churches the tower is always included in the ground-plan, it does not stand apart and tower over the main building but is an integral part of it. Italian Gothic begins late and there are few Gothic buildings in Italy which display the pure style of the French. The Roman, Romanesque and Byzantine continue to influence the Italian style. The ornamentation was inventive, especially in Venice. In the

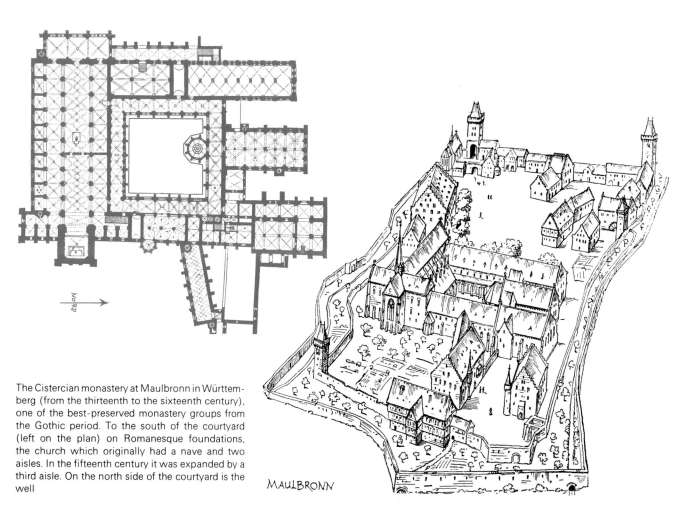

The Cistercian monastery at Maulbronn in Württemberg (from the thirteenth to the sixteenth century), one of the best-preserved monastery groups from the Gothic period. To the south of the courtyard (left on the plan) on Romanesque foundations, the church which originally had a nave and two aisles. In the fifteenth century it was expanded by a third aisle. On the north side of the courtyard is the well

MAULBRONN

60

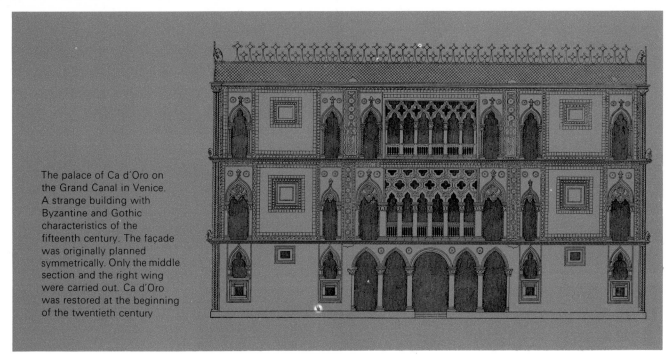

The palace of Ca d'Oro on the Grand Canal in Venice. A strange building with Byzantine and Gothic characteristics of the fifteenth century. The façade was originally planned symmetrically. Only the middle section and the right wing were carried out. Ca d'Oro was restored at the beginning of the twentieth century

secular buildings it is convincing, an integral part of the construction, but often it only seems to be an episode in a long building period.

Florence cathedral, begun in 1296, planned by Arnolfo di Cambio and commissioned by the guild of wool-merchants 'for the honour of the Commune and the people of Florence', was planned entirely as a Gothic building. When it was finished in the first half of the fifteenth century it had, both inside and out, strong cornices in which the horizontal was emphasized, and a dome over the central octagon, an early masterpiece of the early Renaissance, the first great dome in Italy since the Pantheon.

The cathedral in Milan is an example of what happens when, during a too protracted building period, Italian, French and German engineers quarrel among themselves. Nevertheless, Italian Gothic is probably one of the most attractive chapters in architectural history.

German Gothic begins about the middle of the thirteenth century. The best early example is St Elizabeth's church at Marburg, which was built

The church of Santa Maria da Batalha near Lisbon, built by King John of Portugal in 1385

between 1235 and 1283, although the towers were not finished until 1360. In many localities architects were obliged to use brick because of the scarcity of sandstone and good limestone. But brick is not suitable for buttresses. The solution was to resort to hall churches with walls whose pillars project inwards into the church itself. This resulted in the compactness of the body of the building which is characteristic of brick Gothic, and the organization of the sides of the nave into as many niches as the church had windows.

German architects and their patrons quickly adopted the Gothic style; the Romanesque cathedral at Bamberg was begun in 1220; St Elizabeth's church at Marburg only fifteen years later. Northern Gothic contrasts strongly with French and the contrast becomes greater the further the building is from the Rhine.

In Strasbourg there are two influences at work. Leaving aside the Romanesque choir, the transepts and the vault above the crossing, the cathedral is planned entirely in the spirit of the French masters, a building with two towers and an imposing west front. We do not know whether this plan was the work of a French or of a German master, but from 1284 until his death in 1318 Erwin von Steinbach was the architect on the site. A hundred years after his death the north tower was completed by Ulrich von Ensingen and the façade above the rose window was raised by one storey, closing the space between the north tower and the embryo of the south tower.

62

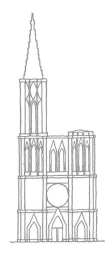

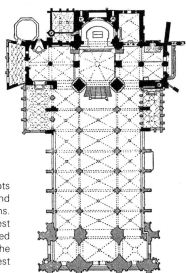

Strasbourg; choir and transepts (black on the ground-plan) stand on eleventh-century foundations. In the two top drawings the west front as planned is contrasted with that as completed. On the right, reconstruction of the west front by Friedrich Adler

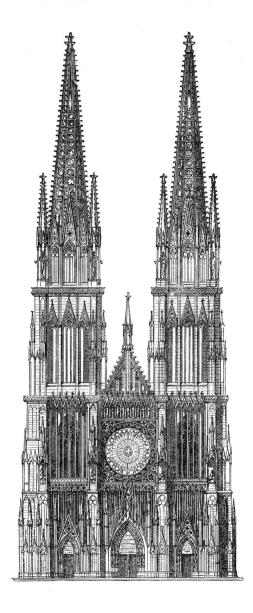

This later addition is usually considered to detract from the effect of the façade, but the world has become accustomed to the strange asymmetry. Through Goethe's essay Master Erwin has received a halo which is perhaps not his by right. But that does not diminish the achievement, and whether the credit should go to a French or to a German master is a question of no great import. Young Goethe's paean is for us dedicated to the Gothic.

To write as Goethe did about Gothic art was at that time unusual; for it was not until 1820, in the Romantic period, that the long-scorned works of the Middle Ages were again recognized in all their greatness. Only in the first half of the nineteenth century were the two great German cathedrals of Ulm and of Cologne completed according to the original plans.

(left) Cologne cathedral; main porch on the western façade
(right) General view of the west front

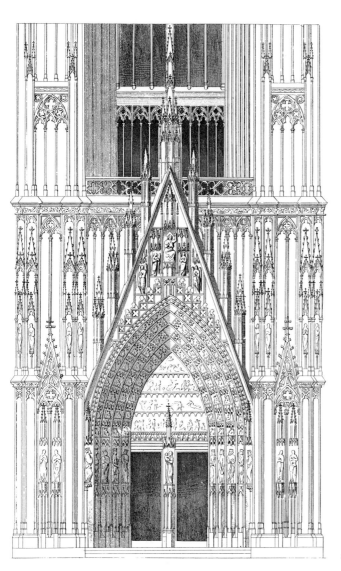

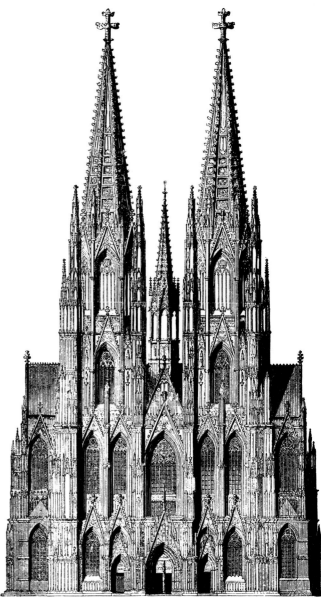

Cologne cathedral, dedicated to St Peter, is also the church of the Three Kings, whose remains are preserved there in a golden shrine. The foundation stone was laid in 1248. Some of the master-builders are known by name: Master Gerhard (died 1279), Master Arnold (died 1308) and his son Johannes (died 1331). The last mediaeval master was Konrad Kuyn (died 1469). But this edifice, which was to be larger and richer than its prototype at Rheims and Amiens, was not completed in the Middle Ages.

By the end of the fifteenth century the choir and part of the nave were finished and the towers had been started. Between these two parts there was a great gap. A crane rose beside the half-finished south tower, and for a long time was a symbol of the city. For fully three centuries the building stayed like this. In 1794 Cologne was occupied by the French, and the decaying cathedral was used as a hay store. The governor of the city even considered pulling the building down altogether.

In the German Romantic period prominent men began to write and to agitate for the completion of the work; among them the philosopher Friedrich Schlegel, the author Joseph Gorres, above all the brothers Sulpiz and Melchior Boisserée, two art lovers whose collection of old German and Flemish masters had made such a profound impression on Goethe.

A plan drawing for the western façade with the two towers was discovered by chance in an old inn in Hesse at the beginning of the century. In 1842 the foundation stone for the new work was laid and in 1880 the work was completed. The director of the building work, Ernst Zwirner, had trained over a hundred stonemasons in Gothic craftsmanship. The cathedral is a masterpiece and a model of the treatment of ancient monuments, but it also demonstrates the limits in the work of restoration: everything in the field of architectural craftsmanship is splendidly successful, but the newly created sculptures cannot begin to compare with those of the original Gothic artists.

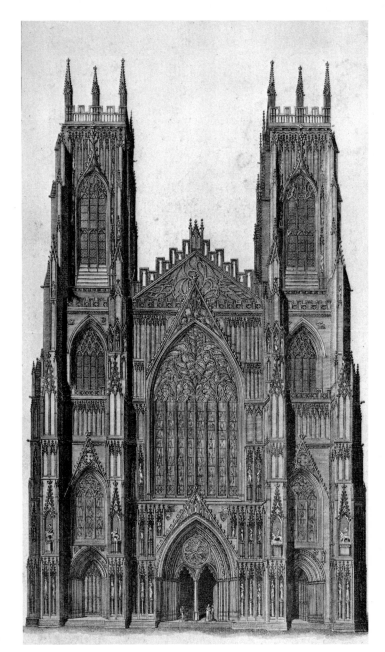

The west front of York Minster

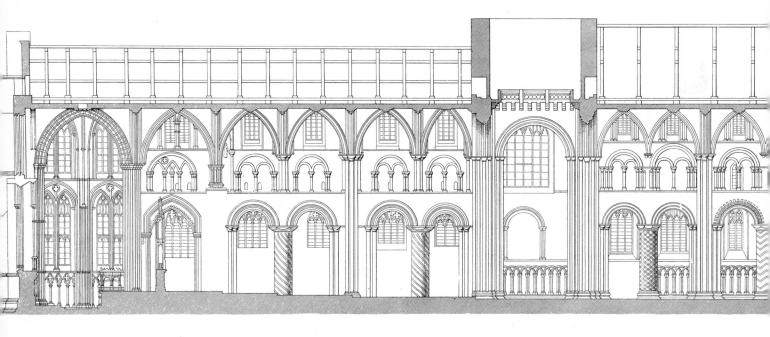

England is sometimes said to be merely the land of late Gothic. This is misleading since English Gothic is barely one generation younger than the French. Even before 1200 the Gothic style was being used in building over Romanesque foundations — in Canterbury, Norwich and elsewhere. In the process, an individual style developed which is differentiated from the French by characteristic arch-constructions often of great technical boldness. Figure-decoration is used sparingly in English cathedrals. But the fanned vaulting is richer in inventiveness and more perfect in technical precision.

With English Gothic one has the impression of looking into stylized treetops with branches of complicated geometric ramifications. No less remarkable is the preference shown for broad window-openings, which allow so much light to enter without destroying the enclosed feeling. The windows are sometimes so wide that it would not be possible to surmount them with a normally proportioned pointed arch. The

solution was the so-called Tudor arch, which is lineally somewhat similar to an Islamic arch. But there the comparison ends, for there is no similarity whatsoever in the tracery.

England found it very difficult to give up the Gothic style, and consequently the Renaissance almost passed England by. The late period, the Tudor Gothic, is probably the most characteristic phase, but the development pointed consistently in this direction. The English have coined good names for their Gothic periods. The early period which is economical in embellishments is called Early English. This style prevails until about 1290. The next hundred years belong to the Decorated style. The name itself indicates the direction of the development: the traceries become richer and the walls are no longer unadorned. Following this is the Perpendicular, so called because of the perpendicular ribs on walls and windows. These are also typical of the Tudor style, but this style also contains features which show a

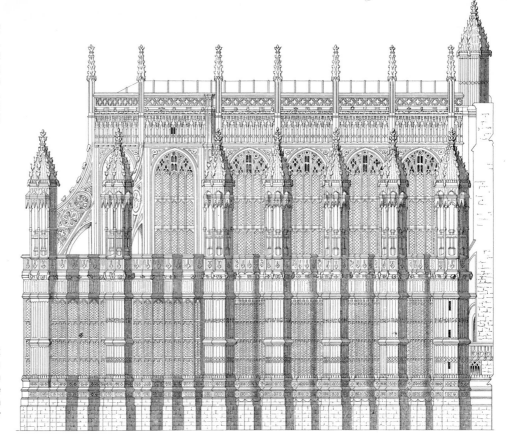

Section through nave and choir of Durham cathedral. On the left, the choir; in the middle the crossing showing the beginning of the tower. The building was planned in the Romanesque style, begun in 1100 and altered and enlarged in the thirteenth and fifteenth centuries

Side view of Henry VI's chapel at Westminster Abbey in London The abbey and episcopal church were begun in the middle of the thirteenth century. The chapel, a fine example of the Perpendicular style, was completed in 1519

departure from the genuine pointed arch: lancet arches, ogee arches and broad Tudor arches. The last epoch is called the Elizabethan. This represents the transition to Renaissance forms, a confusing mixture of old and new.

Around 1600 Gothic ceased to be the language of monumental architecture in England. But the style persisted in country houses and in the residences of noblemen who did not take kindly to the new 'Italianate' style. The style now assumes certain peculiarities, and it is not surprising that through its persistence the strange 'neo-Gothic' of the nineteenth century received stimulation.

The Romantic period, with its admiration of things past, gave rise, both on the Continent and in England, to the sudden outcrop of Gothic town halls, villas

and even artificial ruins. In the second half of the nineteenth century even Gothic railway stations and factories made their appearance. The fashion was short-lived, and may give rise to an amused smile as a manifestation of Romanticism. Nevertheless, the buildings of this period were planned and built with a good deal of artistic understanding and sympathy. The newly discovered Gothic became the style for a lofty idealism and for a paternal town-councillor attitude. This accounts for the many sensitive Gothic church towers and buildings which tourists often take for fifteenth-century buildings; for the imposing Houses of Parliament (1836) on the banks of the Thames; and for the neo-Gothic St Patrick's cathedral in New York.

Representation of the Old World according to the Ptolemaic conception, printed in Nuremberg about 1490, probably the first printed map in a spherical projection. The idea of the world as a globe had long been conjectured, but had not yet been proved. This clumsy woodcut may serve as a symbol for Humanism and the Renaissance, the period in which a new conception of the world began to take shape.

The three continents, Europe, Africa and Asia are shown as well as Libya inferior, Ethiopia inferior and the Indian Ocean (Mare Indicum). Around the globe the winds are designated, among them: *niualis* (snowy); *gelidus* (frosty); *totus calidus* (very warm); and *dat flores* (bringing flowers)

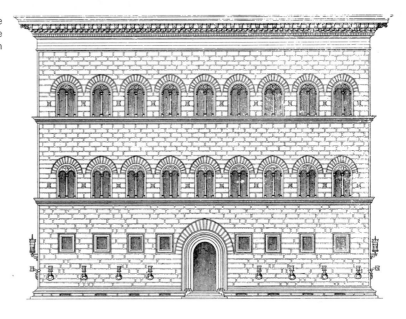

The Strozzi palace in Florence, begun by Benedetto de Majano in 1489 and completed after interruptions in the sixteenth century. The Strozzi were a Florentine patrician family, long antagonists of the mighty Medici family

Renaissance

In the year 1453 Sultan Mohammed II conquered the city and royal residence of Constantinople. Those Greek scholars who were not slain fled to Athens; but three years later Athens itself fell to the Turks and was devastated. The scholars then fled to Italy, settling in Rome, Florence and Bologna, where they taught Greek philosophy. They had brought with them books containing knowledge which in Italy had been partly forgotten, and partly distorted through exegesis and adaptation.

The new intellectuals and their followers called themselves 'humanists'. The word derives from the Latin *humanitas* denoting humaneness, human dignity. From the newly discovered works of antiquity the humanists attempted to formulate a new ideal of culture and intellectual attitudes which were free of the rigid intolerant rules which had grown out of the interpretation of the old writings. The humanists had a difficult task for they aroused the enmity of the clerical dogmatists and were obliged to invent the so-called 'double truth', one aspect of which expressed their own opinions, while the other satisfied the Church Fathers.

In spite of such difficulties intellectual life received an energetic stimulus. Many new universities were founded. Art and literature received fresh impetus. The rebirth of the antique was celebrated, and Hellenistic architectural forms began to supplant everything Gothic.

So this style received its name: rebirth, which is in Italian *rinascimento* and in French *renaissance*. The word was introduced into art history by Vasari. His *rinascita*, however, does not denote a developed style but a continuing process. The word did not come into universal use until 1860 with the appearance of Jacob Burckhardt's book, *The Renaissance in Italy*.

The roots of the Renaissance stretch deep into the Middle Ages. The great following which the humanists found is partially explained by the fact that the ground was already prepared; it had become parched through mediaeval constraint, through reluctance to accept new ideas; where an original thought might have cost a man his head.

'Renaissance' is a word charged with noble implications. It signifies much more than the rediscovery of Hellenistic details, of columns, Corinthian capitals,

of the Roman arch and pillar faced with a pilaster. It means rebirth of the human personality, liberation of the artistic imagination from the rules which were felt to be too rigid, too dry, old and exhausted.

After early hesitations the Church became responsible for great impulses. Pope Nicholas V said he felt like spending all his money on books and buildings. He founded the Vatican library and he thought Old St Peter's had become too small for Christendom. The plans for its enlargement (about 1450) which were completely discarded fifty years later, were his brain-child.

Great initiatives also came from the new wealthy patrons: the princes, the rich merchants, and not least from the rulers of the Italian city-republics.

It is to be noted that the change was easier for the artists and architects than for the thinkers. During the whole of the sixteenth century it was not advisable to propound new ideas too publicly. The trials of Giordano Bruno and Galileo Galilei, who proclaimed a new view of the universe and a new astronomy, illimitable and with innumerable suns, came not at the beginning of the Renaissance but at the end of the epoch. Giordano was burnt at the stake in 1600, after long imprisonment, and Galileo was forced to recant to save his life in 1633. The rebirth was not one moment in time but a gradual, painful awakening, often under the shadow of the Inquisition.

The new building style originated in Italy. The epoch opens in 1420 with a resolute rejection of everything which later came to be called *gotico*. But the return to old Roman and Hellenic building styles did not result in a mere faithful copying. To the old columns and arches there were added a preference for the centralized building, for the unbroken façade, a new feeling for space and a new 'taste'. The feeling that prompted the new patron seems to have been: display your wealth, your artistic knowledge, your pride, your vanity, but see that the finished building adequately and justly serves its purpose, and build a house in which you can live comfortably and in which people don't have to come up narrow spiral

70

staircases to a room sparsely lit by wall-slits; arrange your windows in an order which reflects the order of your thinking; show the genuinely solid structure of your walls and build them so strong that they do not require buttresses. Every house rises in storeys, one above the other; build your house so that this is evident from outside. Let cornices run above and below the windows. Emphasize the roof-cornice strongly, so that people can see that your money hadn't run out before the job was done, etc.

On these and similar principles, large and small Renaissance palaces grew up, as well as ordinary houses; at first sparing in ornamentation, later ingeniously overloaded; then seeking to emphasize the perpendicular lines of the façade with projecting pillars or with pilasters, without weakening the effect of the horizontal cornices. Thus every Renaissance façade follows a perpendicular and a horizontal arrangement to achieve a satisfactory proportion.

San Zaccaria, the oldest Renaissance church in Venice, begun in 1450 by Antonio Gambello. Façade by Moro Caducci about 1515

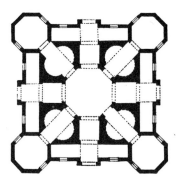

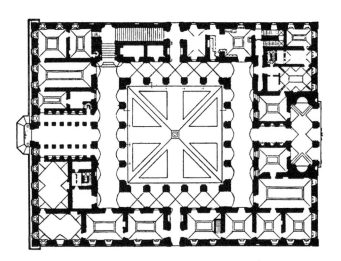

Two ground-plans: on the left, an idea for a church with the axes of a double cross, designed by Antonio Filarete in 1460. On the right, a plan for the Palazzo Farnese in Rome by Antonio de Sangallo the younger about 1530

71

Golden Section in the Tempietto of Donato d'Angelo Bramante (1502). The rectangles over the drawing of the round temple are 'golden'. The Tempietto, a pure central building, stands in the monastery courtyard of S. Pietro in Montorio in Rome

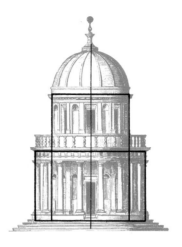

Something should be said here of the *sectio aurea*, the 'Golden Section', according to which great numbers of diagrams are made, showing pictures and buildings, ground-plans, façades, leaves and flowers — all overlaid with seemingly mysterious geometrical lines and arcs and furnished with detailed explanations. Sometimes more mystery is read into these conclusions than the subject will stand.

The Golden Section is the division of a line into two parts so that the length of the whole bears the same relationship to the longer part as the longer does to the shorter. This may sound confusing, but a glance at the diagram will make it clear. There are several methods of determining the division. The simplest is as follows: the length to be divided is considered as the long side of a right-angled triangle, the shorter side of which is half that length. With the compass an arc is drawn from one end of the hypotenuse intersecting the hypotenuse at a point equal to the length of the short side. From this point of intersection a second arc is drawn with centre at the other end of the hypotenuse intersecting the long side and so dividing this side into two unequal parts, major and minor, which stand in a golden relationship to each other. The relationship between the two is the same as that of the major to the sum of major and minor. A rectangle constructed with these two measurements is a 'Golden Rectangle'.

The golden division can also be arrived at mathematically and is expressed as: $y = 0.61803\ldots$ It is

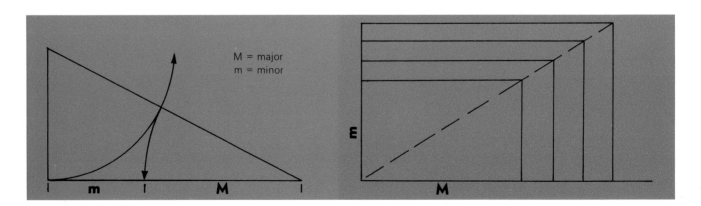

enough to know that a rectangle whose sides are in the relationship of 3 to 5 is virtually a Golden Rectangle, not mathematically precise but near enough for the naked eye. The discrepancy would be even smaller if the series were continued: 5 to 8; 8 to 13; 13 to 21; 21 to 34; 34 to 55; 55 to 89; 89 to 144 and so on. The reader will notice that the sum of any two ratio-numbers produces the second number for the next golden relationship.

The *sectio aurea* was not invented during the Renaissance. It had been a part of the history of architecture since the earliest times, and certainly since Euclid (about 300 B.C.) who is thought to have discovered the exact construction of the pentagon, which bears considerable correspondence to the Golden Section. The sides of the five-pointed star, pentagram or druid's foot, are divided at their points of intersection in a golden relationship. There are other remarkable correspondences which no doubt explain why the pentagram is regarded as a magical symbol, potent against witches, also why it is used as a symbol by secret societies.

Golden Sections can be demonstrated on innumerable buildings, as well as in the composition of pictures. But the play of numbers and compass lines should not be exaggerated. Good scale and harmony of proportion cannot be explained by numbers alone. At best formulas only go part of the way towards explaining the creations of genius. The Renaissance was obsessed with the formulation of a theory of perfection. But this search for a theory was only an accompaniment to the act of creation.

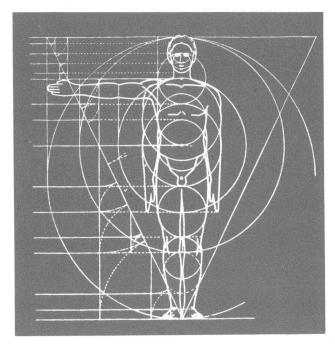

Golden Section and the human figure

Five golden rectangles produced by the intersection of two superimposed pentagrams

The Renaissance began to spread across Europe at the same time that it began to decline in Italy. At the beginning of the sixteenth century it reached France, then it crossed the Alps.

Understandably it was not adopted in all the European countries in its original clarity of form but in its ornate flowering period, when it was occasionally 'too much of a good thing'. However, it frequently appears in a wise moderation and with a distinct desire to avoid the obviously Italianate element. It became the style of the international merchants' houses, of the serried façades of the mercantile depots, of the multi-storeyed gables of town halls — manifold representation of a period of prosperous bourgeoisie, innocent of any foreboding of the ravages of war and distress which were to change the picture in the seventeenth century.

The decline of the Renaissance is called 'Mannerism', which is derived from *manier* signifying 'style'. It is intended to imply a highly personal method of ex-

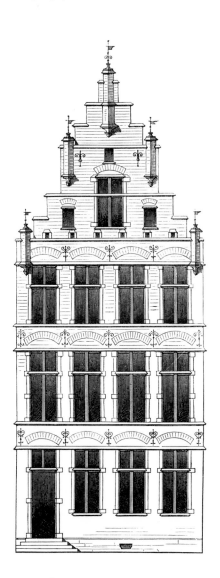

(left) The Armoury in Danzig built about 1600, destroyed in 1945
(right) Merchant's house in Antwerp, built 1580

74

pression, and also the adoption of the personal style of one master by another or by a school. Full justice is not done to the conception of Mannerism by this explanation, for Mannerism implies at the same time an excessive, too artificial, play with all available resources. It tends towards exaggeration, to tricks of perspective, to theatrical effects. But this is not all, for the style has no definable limits. It is the outcome of a spiritually hesitant period which, disturbed by the Reformation and the Counter-Reformation, ought to have sought new attitudes but preferred to come to terms with familiar forms and attitudes and to solve its problems by imaginative variations and exaggerations.

The term 'Mannerism' is like other -isms: not specifically fixed in the time scale. It represents an attitude, like Classicism, Archaism, Historicism; an approach which is not free, which hankers after that which is creatively exhausted. But in its uncertainties it already gives notice of new things to come.

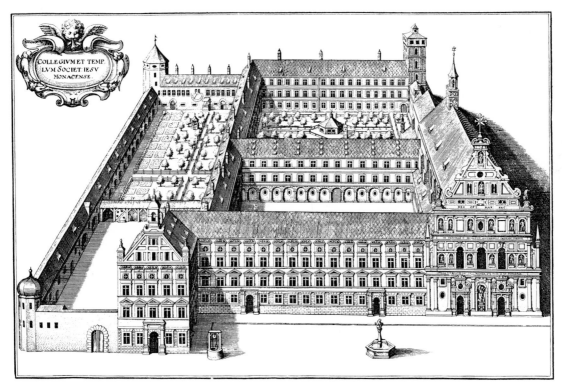

Example of a monastic settlement of the sixteenth century — the Jesuit college in Munich
On the right is St Michael's church, completed in 1595 (from Merian's *Topographia Bavariae*)

Palazzo Valmarano in Vicenza, a work of Andrea Palladio, completed 1566. Palladio is the creator of the style named after him, Palladian Classicism, which appeared towards the end of the Renaissance and led to the Baroque. He used almost exclusively Romano-Hellenistic building motifs, which he freely subjected to the new-found desire for display. Typical of many of his buildings is the 'Colossal Order', a system of façade arrangement in which dominating columns or pillars link several storeys

Baroque and Rococo

Pearls which were not perfectly round were called *barocco* by the Portuguese and Italians, *barock* by the Germans, and *baroque* by the French. In time 'baroque' came to mean 'bizarre'. In the nineteenth century it became the acknowledged description of the style which began to supersede the Renaissance about 1600. Used at first to describe only a kind of architecture, it soon became the term for a distinctive style in all the arts and so, figuratively, a description of a way of life which expressed itself in physically sweeping gestures, which preferred exuberantly rounded human figures, and which in its joy in the use of curved lines ran the danger of becoming turgid, bombastic and debasing.

For the three successive styles: Gothic, Renaissance and Baroque, we might use three goddesses as symbolic figures: Diana, Juno and Venus. The first, Diana, the huntress, the moon-woman, protectress of virgins, is slim and dainty and, in spite of her athletic pursuits, is maidenly and reserved to the point of coyness. The second, Juno, is statuesque and voluptuous, but her stateliness makes her not quite so attractive to men as Diana or as the third goddess, Venus, in whose image are intermingled notions of femininity, beauty and sensuality.

Another interpretation is that Gothic sees life as Fate, (Destiny); the Renaissance sees it as a problem; the Baroque sees it as Joy. But these comparisons are merely games: they illustrate a reality but never express it completely.

The Baroque may be assigned the period 1600 to 1760 although the year 1600 must not be taken as a specific starting-point. The Baroque grew out of the Renaissance through the stage we call Mannerism. There is no exact turning-point. The fundamental forms, which were fixed, began to strive towards a new harmony, to overflow one into the other, to disguise their constructive textures, to simulate with a smile, or even a loud laugh. The limits of each art become confused: architecture fuses into sculpture, sculpture into architecture. And painting is no longer the two-dimensional decoration of an interior, but the promoter and abettor of perspective effects: domes, barrel-vaults, and ceilings become visions of heaven, cloud-scapes of allegorical events for which the largest space would be too small if its frontiers were not extended by the painter's art.

For the interaction of the arts of architecture, sculp-

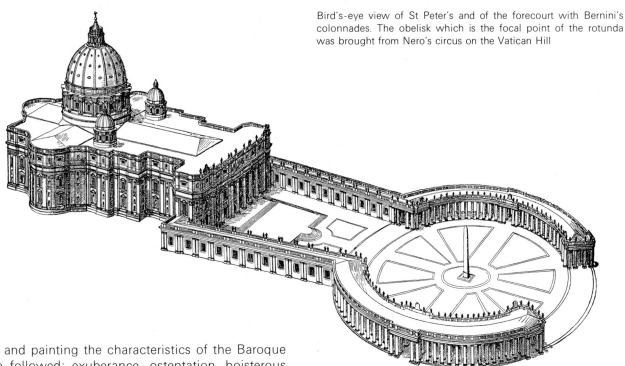

Bird's-eye view of St Peter's and of the forecourt with Bernini's colonnades. The obelisk which is the focal point of the rotunda was brought from Nero's circus on the Vatican Hill

ture and painting the characteristics of the Baroque style followed: exuberance, ostentation, boisterous profusion.

A short summary of the building history of St Peter's in Rome shows how the Baroque — here as elsewhere — grew out of the Renaissance.

Pope Nicholas V planned the expansion of the old basilica in 1450. The building of a new choir began outside the existing church. In 1506 under Pope Julius II Donato d'Angelo Bramante planned a building in the form of a Greek cross with a central dome, subsidiary domes and with barrel-vaults roofing the aisles.

In 1515 Raphael (Raffaello Santi) took over the planning and the direction of the building under Pope Leo X. The first arcades of the south transept were vaulted. However, only five years were granted to Raphael. He died at the age of thirty-seven and was awarded an honoured resting-place in the Pantheon. In 1520 Antonio Sangello took charge of the building for twenty-six years — the apses were built, the floor-level was raised by over three yards, and a new project for the domes was discussed but never started.

Ground-plan of St Peter's according to Michelangelo's plan of 1547, which was influenced by Bramante's plan. In the seventeenth century the plan was altered by bringing the façade forward to create a larger interior

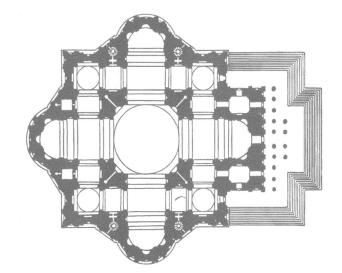

77

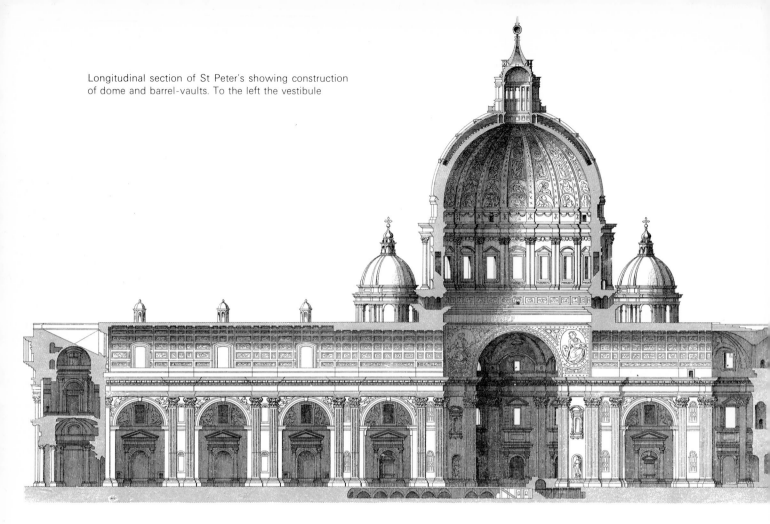

Longitudinal section of St Peter's showing construction of dome and barrel-vaults. To the left the vestibule

In 1547, under Pope Paul III, the general direction was assumed by Michelangelo Buonarotti. The area was decreased. The south apses were torn down. A new plan for the façade was adopted. Yet a third solution for the domes was planned. After Michelangelo's death in 1564 the building went ahead virtually according to his plans until 1573. Then there was a standstill for twelve years.

In 1585, Pope Sixtus V delegated the work to Giacomo della Porta and Domenico Fontana. The plan for the domes was changed again, and the building was extended to the east in order to connect it to the Vatican. In 1592 the dome was finished and the construction of the interior began. From 1607 till 1629 Carlo Maderna continued the work under Pope Paul V. Maderna, a pupil of Fontana, can already

be considered an artist of the Baroque, but nevertheless he conformed to Michelangelo's ideas more than his predecessors. The Pope wanted two side chapels, and to make this possible the exterior had to be modified. This proved to be disadvantageous to the façade, at whose extreme ends two west front towers were planned. This raised the difficult problem of the final form of the façade.

In 1626, the interior decoration being finished, the church was consecrated.

In 1646 Lorenzo Bernini made an attempt to build the two western towers but the foundations proved to be unequal to the extra burden.

In 1696 Andreas Schluter of Danzig took over. The impressive ornamentation of the façade is his — especially famous are the heads of warriors on the

The church of St Agnes on the Piazza Navona in Rome, built 1652–77 by Girolamo and Carlo Rainaldi. Borromini also worked here during the first five years. The façade is slightly curved and ingeniously divided into five main axes

A B A C A D A D A C A B A

Portal scheme of St Agnes. The five main axes: B C D C B, separated by similar pairs of pillars (A)

INNOCENTIVS X.
PONT MAX AN VI

INNOCENTIVS X.
PONT. MAX.
LATERANENSEM BASILICAM
CONSTANTINI MAGNI IMPERATORIS
RELIGIONE AC MVNIFICENTIA EXTRVCTAM
SVMMORVMQVE PONTIFICVM PIETATE
SAEPIVS INSTAVRATAM
VETVSTATE IAM FATISCENTEM
NOVA MOLITIONE ADVETEREM
EXPARTE ADHVC STANTEM CONFORMATAM
ORNATV SPLENDIDIORE RESTITVIT
ANNO IVBILAEI MDCL PONT. VI.

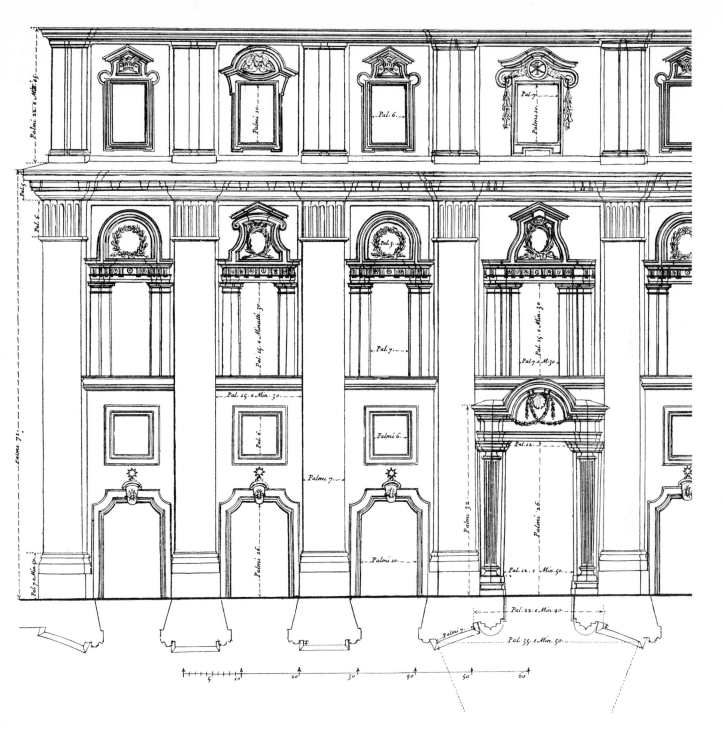

Borromini's decoration in the Roman church of St John Lateran with the coat of arms of Pope Innocent X

Drawing after Borromini's plans for the Collegio di Propaganda Fide in Rome

(left) The church of SS. Martin and Luke erected on the foundations
of an ancient Roman building on the Forum Romanum. The design
was by Pietro Cortona, a contemporary of Borromini

(top right) The side façade of the Library of St Mark's on St Mark's
Square in Venice, by Jacopo Sansovino, 1553

(bottom right) The portal façade of the church of S. Giorgio de
Greci in Venice, also by Jacopo Sansovino, 1532

82

THE LOUVRE

There has been a castle on the banks of the Seine since the thirteenth century. It was enlarged by Francis I and dismantled by Charles V. In 1546 a new palace was begun by Pierre Lescot and Jean Goujon, continued after 1600 by Jacques Lemercier. The façade here shown was planned and executed under Louis XIV. The king called Bernini to Paris but they could not reach agreement. Then Claude Perrault designed a classicistic-palladian plan which was executed during the years 1667–74. The façade is dominated by sixteen pairs of Corinthian columns. The middle section of the façade is a fine intensification of the axial arrangement indicated on each wing. During the French Revolution the art treasures of the Louvre were declared national property and the gallery was opened to the public

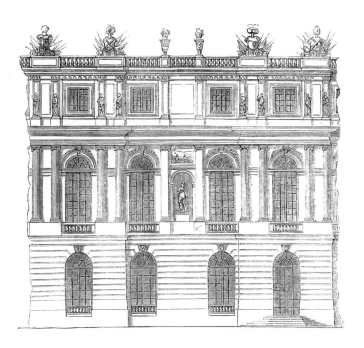

VERSAILLES

Part of the façade of the great palace built under Louis XIV in a park in which there had previously been only a small hunting lodge. In 1668 the building was begun by the architects Louis and François LeVan, and after 1676 continued by Jules Hardouin-Mansart

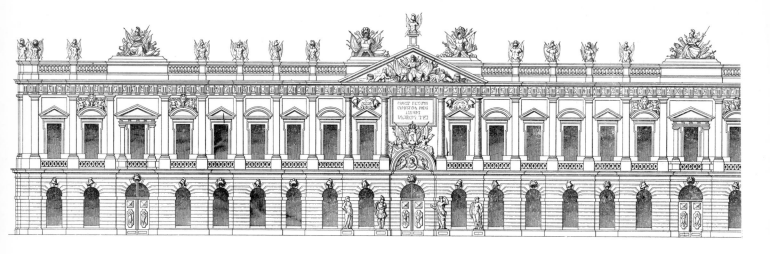

THE ARMOURY IN BERLIN
The plan is by Johann Arnold Nering, who is first mentioned in 1684 as chief engineer to the prince-elector. The Armoury is the first of a series of monumental buildings under Frederick III. Nering also drew up the building plans for 'Friedrichstadt', the first planned residential quarter in Berlin. When Nering died in 1695 almost 300 houses already stood finished according to his plans and to his ideas

WÜRZBURG
From an eighteenth-century engraving. The town palace of the prince-bishop begun in 1719 under Johann Philipp Franz von Schönborn. The plan of the whole layout is by Maximilian von Welsch. Technical direction was in the hands of the engineer and captain of artillery Balthasar Neumann. In 1744 the structure was finished, in 1770 the interior decoration. The Paris architects Boffrand and de Cotte co-operated as expert advisers. Lukas von Hildebrandt came from Vienna, and from Venice came the Tiepolos, father and son, who created the frescoes in the Imperial Hall and on the ceiling of the Great Staircase

MELK ON THE DANUBE

The Benedictine abbey towers high over the town and the river on a steep granite outcrop. Jakob Prandtauer was the master-builder. Begun in 1702 the building was finished ten years later. Prandtauer ranks with Fischer von Erlach as the fertilizing mind behind Danubian Baroque. Melk is distinguished not only by its magnificent position in the landscape but also by the airy height of its interiors and the delicacy of its decorated façade. The drawing on the right shows the elevation of the main façade with its towers, and behind these the high dome. The adjacent sketches illustrate the ground-plan of the towers

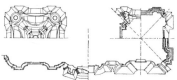

WEINGARTEN

In Suabia, from an engraving of 1723. Only one part of this attractive plan was carried out. Building was begun in 1715. In 1724 the church was finished; work on the monastery went on for some years longer. The symmetrical semicircular gardens and the domestic buildings were never started

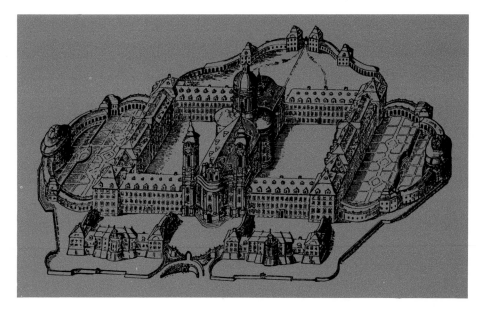

85

keystones of the window arches. Schluter was primarily a sculptor and among other works he created the equestrian statue of the Great Elector (1700). He became director of the Berlin Academy, but fell into disgrace in 1706 when the Mint Tower which he had designed threatened to collapse when the building was almost finished.

The Baroque is the art style of Catholic countries; it typifies the rejuvenation which was produced by the Counter-Reformation.

But the secular buildings of the Baroque period are a symbol of worldly absolutism; the art of great princes. Because of the great expenditure involved, they only too often proved disastrous to the lesser princes who emulated them. In its last period, the Rococo, the style became reduced in scale, moving towards rather frivolous variants. It could be adopted with fewer misgivings, not only by the less opulent princes but also by the bourgeoisie.

'Rococo' is a playful, eminently suitable, modification of the French *rocaille* meaning 'shell-work'. One might also coin the phrase: 'loop-work'. This would describe a constantly recurring decorative motif both in the painting and in the stucco-work. And this already indicates that we are dealing with a feature eminently suited to interior decoration.

Longitudinal section
through the collegiate
library at Altenburg,
omitting the roof

The Baroque principles of building were taken over in the Rococo style but on a reduced scale. The oval ground-plan is found more frequently, and corresponding to this the so-called basket-arch: a shallow elliptical vault based on three circles. Both give a lighter effect to the finished building.

In this style everything is curved, but as a form of decoration rather than as a technical necessity. In fact, cupolas are often only there for the sake of appearances, mere screens of plaster over wire-netting to conceal the roof-rafters above.

The Rococo was French, just as the early Renaissance was Italian. The French, however, seldom use the word. They prefer greater accuracy and divide the age of elegance into three periods. The initial period they call 'Regence', and is the period of the regency of Philippe of Orleans (1715—23). The next short period is called 'Louis Quinze' after the king of that name. The third period, already showing the transition to neo-Classicism, is called 'Louis Seize' after his grandson and successor. The fate of Louis XVI accords grimly with the gay mood of the Rococo.

He was a modest man who recognized the mistakes of his predecessors and was committed to reforms for the good of his people. But to no avail. He died in 1793 on the guillotine, that ingenious red-painted framework, which removed heads so efficiently.

Even more than in the land of its origin, German and Austrian Rococo influenced changes in the exterior of buildings. Façades are often delicately curved, otherwise sparing in architectural features, but ornamented with fine stucco-work. Among many other perfect examples, both exterior and interior, are the small palaces in the Nymphenburg Park in Munich and Frederick II's Sans Souci at Potsdam. German patrons often called in French and Italian architects, but the work of the German artists is not inferior to that of their famous colleagues.

The churches in Bavaria and Austria are examples of how such a worldly, light-hearted and vivacious style, with its tumbling cherubs, only too obviously children of the earth, can also be solemn in its own inspired way: a hymn of praise sung by many voices in ringing tones.

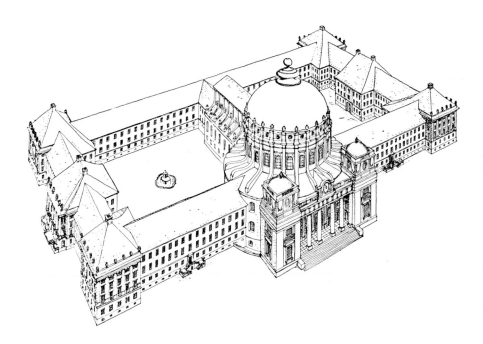

SAINT BLASIEN
In the Black Forest. Bird's-eye view omitting the surrounding park. The building was designed by the Alsatian architect Jean d'Ixnard, and was completed in 1783. Agitated Baroque forms are dispensed with, especially on the portal front of the church. The rectilinear tendencies of Classicism are foreshadowed

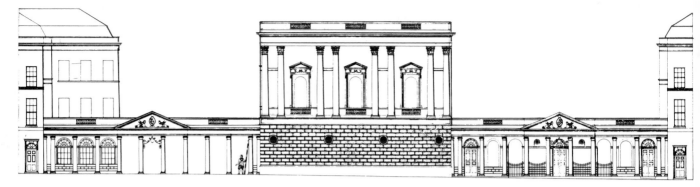

Neo-Classicism

It is a controversial point, when and to what extent the early English Classicism of the seventeenth century made its impact on the Continent. France was in the throes of Absolutism, Germany was at war, and Italy was in the process of losing its predominant position in European culture, content with the laurels gained by its great monuments of former times. None of these countries had any particular points of contact with England.

In 1600 the young Englishman Inigo Jones (1573–1652) travelled through northern Italy and brought back, besides many travel sketches, the book *Architettura* by Andrea Palladio, the great architect of the late Renaissance who had probably studied Vitruvius better than anybody else. Palladio (1508–80) was the father of the so-called 'Colossal Order', a principle in façade design in which dominant columns or pilasters stretch over several storeys.

At the same time that Jones was in Italy, a young German was there also studying the architecture of Palladio. He was Elias Holl of Augsburg (1573–1646). The two men did not meet. Holl was appointed civic architect to the city of Augsburg in 1602 and that year he built his masterpiece, the city armoury. Ten years later he built the town hall, bold and severe in the clarity of its façade — a thoroughly personal variant of all he had seen in Italy. Both works belong to the finest creations of the German Renaissance.

Palladio's effect on Inigo Jones was totally different. It helped him to anticipate the style which was to develop in other countries only after the Baroque and the Rococo had run their course.

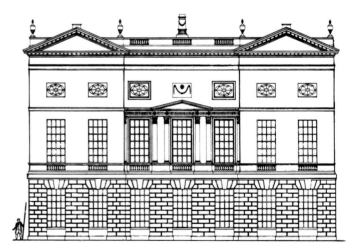

The Guild Hall built by Thomas Baldwin in 1740. Like the Royal Crescent this building was erected as a contribution to John Wood's town plan for the famous spa

88

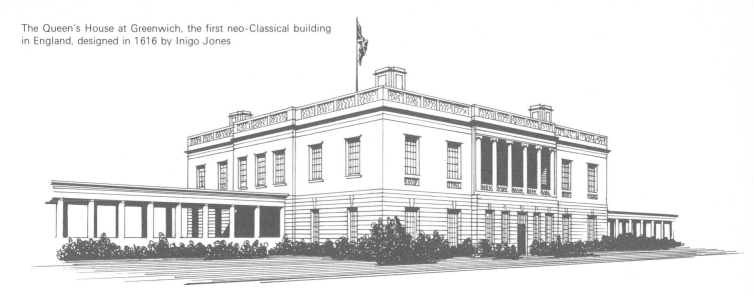

The Queen's House at Greenwich, the first neo-Classical building in England, designed in 1616 by Inigo Jones

If one compares Jones's Queen's House in Greenwich (begun in 1616) with buildings which were produced in England 150 years later, one observes that the stylistic differences are of the most minor character. English neo-Classicism does not begin with Inigo Jones in the time scale, but it found in him its great prototype.

Conditions in England in the first half of the seventeenth century were not sufficiently peaceful to encourage building, let alone the translation of Palladio into English terms. Charles I, grandson of Mary Queen of Scots, startled his subjects, both English and Scots, by his decision that Parliament was unnecessary and that he could rule by himself.

Aston Hall in Warwickshire, built in 1630 by John Thorpe in the Elizabethan style

89

St Paul's cathedral, the most important of Christopher Wren's many London churches. The left half of the drawing shows a section through the transverse axis. Here the sloping colonnade can be seen which supports the inner dome. Above this there is a cone-shaped roof of masonry on which rests the rafters which support the outer dome. The latter is crowned by a double lantern. The cross is 336 feet above the floor of the church

This obviously could come to no good end. After victorious battles under Oliver Cromwell's leadership against the Royalists, the Puritans declared a republic. Charles was beheaded in 1649. Cromwell's republic came to grief because of the incompetence of his followers in home affairs. The Stuarts returned, having learned nothing in the meantime. Then came the Plague (1665) followed by the Great Fire (1666). Not until the Dutchman, William of Orange, married to a Stuart princess, ascended the English throne did times in England begin to improve.

The eighteenth century was a great one for England. Overseas possessions were consolidated in India, Canada and Australia and hundreds of intermediate bases were established on islands and on the great maritime highways. England became the motherland of a new epoch: the 'Age of Enlightenment' during which the principle was established that if people held differing beliefs, it was not necessary to crack their skulls.

Christopher Wren (1632–1723) built fifty-five new churches in London alone following the Great Fire — among them St Paul's Cathedral. The dome of St Paul's is considered perfect, but it crowns a building which turns with some hesitation from the Baroque to Palladian Classicism, just as does the Invalides in Paris (1706).

On the time-chart the beginning of Classicism on the Continent is relegated to the last quarter of the eighteenth century. In France there was revolution; and according to a later Russian formulation, revolution means:

> 'The swift collapse within a few years of institutions which have required centuries to take root, and seem so secure and unshakable that even the most audacious reformers hardly venture to attack them in their writings. Revolution signifies the crumbling or collapse of all which up to then had formed the essential content of the social, religious, political and economic life of a people.'

Compared with France, the end of the eighteenth century in Germany was not so stormy, above all, not so bloody. The Seven Years War had ended. There was some antagonism against the lesser princes, who

The former Arch at Euston Station, London

attempted to match the Sun-King in the squandering of tax-money and who, when their coffers were empty, sent their recruiting officers to press-gang young men into the army in order to sell them in whole companies. New ideas at that time were generated in Germany not through politics but through literature.

Sturm und Drang (Storm and Stress) was soon coined as the name for this new poetical movement. It was the title of a play which had been written in 1776 by Friedrich Maximilian Klinger, a 'firebrand' who later became an officer under a variety of masters, and died as commander of the Russian Cadet Corps.

Out of the period of 'Storm and Stress' there grew the epoch of 'Romanticism'. This is the movement among the painters and poets which was contemporary with neo-Classicism and influenced the transition of the latter through 'neo-Gothic' to pure 'Historicism' (imitation of past styles).

In Goethe's essay 'On German architecture' neo-Classicism is discussed. He does not use that term, and what he thinks of it is undoubtedly the reaction to the unexpected impression which he had experienced on seeing Strasbourg Cathedral.

He has little good to say of neo-Classicism. The 'Storm and Stress' of his youth tempt him to look back, in a survey committed to passionate and enthusiastic sentences, across the intervening centuries, to the time when a house consisted of four walls constructed of honest masonry, not a building of columns whose intermediate spaces were filled up with brick or stonework.

It displeased him to see features from the ancient temples being used everywhere in the construction of ordinary citizens' houses. He valued antiquity too

91

highly to stand by and see it profaned. Goethe, who not only observed the revolution in taste but participated in it, was forced to recognize that the rediscovery of the Classical was not the point of departure for new ideas and impulses, but the consequence of a new feeling for life, of an inner urge to sweep away the Baroque with all its florid ornamentation.

What displeased Goethe, and was also the criticism of later commentators on the neo-Classical was, above all, that the architects used a language of forms which was far-fetched and had become archaic, and that classical elements, which had been conceived as fitting for the representation of the loftiest things, were being used for buildings whose purpose could in no way be compared with a temple in honour of Zeus.

For instance: a small dwelling-house would be equipped with a miniature porch — Doric, Ionic or Corinthian — which was to be used as an entrance, or exit, not for a priest or for the dedicated faithful, but just for ordinary people.

The difference between the Classical and the neo-Classical can be quite simply stated: the Classical was never concerned with the problems of everyday

Schinkel's diagrammatic drawing for the Museum of Classical Art (Altes Museum) in Berlin, showing the colonnade stretching across the entire front. The building looks on to the Lustgarten (pleasure garden). In the foreground the Kupfergarten canal of the river Spree. The Lustgarten is today called Marx-Engels Platz. Facing the museum lay the royal palace which was demolished after the Second World War (p. 92)

Thomas U. Walter's Girard Institute in Philadelphia. An example of the Greek Revival style in the United States of America.

life; whereas these are the main concerns of the neo-Classical.

German neo-Classical attained its highest achievements in the work of Karl Friedrich Schinkel (1781–1841), painter and architect from Neu-Ruppin. He was a pupil at the Berlin Academy of Architecture under Friedrich Gilly, the great initiator of neo-Classicism, not one of whose few buildings has survived. In his twenties Schinkel travelled to France and Italy, and in 1815 he was appointed head of the Office of Works to the king of Prussia. He had a feeling for form and an extremely sharp perception for good proportions. He loved Doric columns. With them, he could do everything: the royal guard-house in Berlin (1816); the country villa, Schloss Charlottenhof near Potsdam (1826). Of his many buildings may be mentioned: the Schauspielhaus (theatre) in Berlin (1821) with an Ionic portico; the Old Museum in Berlin (1830); the Nikolai church in Potsdam (1837). Among his plans were the building of a new royal palace on the Acropolis at Athens; the building of a palace, Orianda, in the Crimea for the empress of Russia; as well as churches, in Romanesque, Byzantine and Gothic styles.

The Hall of Fame on the Theresienhill in Munich, erected by Leo von Klenze in the Doric order in 1834–53. In the middle of the open rectangle the statue of Bavaria by Ludwig Schwantalher; to provide the bronze casting for this statue several valuable sixteenth- and seventeenth-century statues were melted down

Such ideas already proclaim the Historicism of the second half of the nineteenth century. With Schinkel there was moderation, no pomp, no ostentation; but later the same ideas spread with an unrestrained excess.

While King Ludwig I of Bavaria was still crown prince he cherished a plan to build a forum on classical lines on the western periphery of the capital city of Munich. The result is one of the finest examples of what the transformation of Greek and Hellenistic ideas are capable of achieving under northern skies. Leo von Klenze (1784–1864) built the western portal to this square (called the Propylaen after its prototype on the Acropolis) in the Doric order; and for the museum building on the south side of the square he used the Ionic-Hellenistic. The museum on the north side was designed by Georg Friedrich Ziebland (1800–73) with a raised portico of eight Corinthian columns. It was part of the project of the king and his architects that on the eastern side of the square, the town itself should expand to complete the square. The idea was that the Forum of 'Isar-Athens' should also have a civic side.

Neo-Classicism, which had begun with so much promise, gave way eventually to Historicism, which for fifty years only produced 'castles of confectionery'. On looking back, it is easy to see why neo-Classicism received various names for its short periods in the various countries of its adoption.

In England the Inigo Jones period is called 'English Classical' while the second real period (about 1730–1850) is called the 'Classical Revival'.

In France the period begins as 'Directoire' (1795–1805), the name of the revolutionary government. This is followed by 'Empire' after the Napoleonic empire (until 1814). This style persisted after the Napoleonic period for a couple of decades, but was overwhelmed about the middle of the century by Historicism. The same fate befell German neo-Classicism at the same time, as already foreshadowed in Schinkel's work.

Things had come thus far. The neo-Classical was now only capable of expressing the dignity of modest presumptions. But in its new-found modesty it was much too noble for the grandiloquent character of the period which had called it into being.

It seems as though the critics had foreseen what would happen when the desire for 'show' spread further, and when the artists remained barren of new ideas or individuality. They had to fall back on past styles; not on the style of any particular epoch, but on a concoction of all styles mixed together from all epochs: Egyptian, Byzantine, Romanesque, Gothic and so on.

Historicism is the name given to this arrogant hotch-potch of all that was historic, good and costly. There is hardly a large city anywhere where one does not see standing around typical monuments of the monument-mad second half of the nineteenth century, an age of total creative barrenness. A Doric colonnade on a hill, dwarfed by a gigantic female figure; neo-Gothic castles on mountain tops; the so-called Crystal Palace in London; a neo-Baroque cathedral in Berlin, botched together with decorative elements from a dozen different prototypes; domes of a

The Arc de Triomphe in Paris, begun in 1806 by Jean-François Chalgrin in honour of Napoleon I, but only completed thirty years later under King Louis Philippe I. Since the end of the First World War, the body of an unknown soldier rests beneath the arch

Pantheon-like scale over booking-offices; opera-houses like sugar castles, in which the theatrical performance begins with the exterior façade, continues with flamboyant pomp into the foyer, into the corridors, as far as the royal box — but breaks off abruptly with the staircases leading up to the upper tiers.

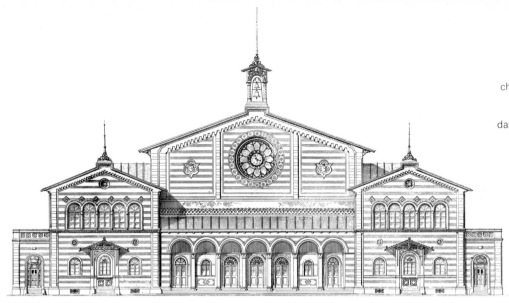

Technically this was all well executed and durable. And the technical possibilities led to trickery — stucco corbels were suspended from disguised iron brackets, looking as though they might bear any burden the world cared to load them with, whereas in actual fact they were hollow.

A new material was being used for building elements: cast iron. Anything could now be made of cast iron, moreover it could be mass produced: Corinthian capitals, Arabic window-gratings, Gothic tracery.

The gay city of Paris wanted to have a tower higher than any that had yet been built. The engineer, Alexandre Gustave Eiffel, built them one of iron, nearly 1,000 feet high. Although it is not exactly a thing of beauty, the Eiffel Tower is at least one of the few honest buildings of this period.

A neo-Gothic country house near London (1873)

Façade of the photographic studio 'Elvira' in Munich. A dragon-like fantasy of reddish-gold stucco on a green background, designed by August Endell in 1898. The house was demolished in 1936 as being out of harmony with the general tone of the street

Art Nouveau

At the end of the nineteenth century something fresh was in the air. New impulses came from the painters, the book-illustrators and the artistic craftsmen. It is not possible to say exactly where it began. At various places groups of artists withdrew into the country because they found the stucco and the plush of the metropolitan cities hideous. In several countries groups of artists or art-minded people founded magazines: in France the *Revue Blanche* (1891); in England Charles Holme started the *Studio* (1893); in Germany *Youth* (1895). No new style was as yet proclaimed, but there was condemnation of the old style, the Historicism which was a threat to anything new. And in time something new emerged as if automatically.

The painter Cuno Amiet (1868–1961) of Solothurn writes in 1893 of his stay in the Breton artists' village of Pont-Aven and of the artists at work there: 'Everything was new; remarkable, fantastic people, animals, trees, houses, luminous colours unknown to me, line-drawing which united the human body with

its surroundings in the most improbable way.'

The new style showed itself first in painting, in book-illustration, in ornamental borders for book-printing; then it began to influence furniture, cutlery, vases, stair-carpets and finally — if after some hesitation — façades.

Its typical expression is a curve: a rising line which bends to the left, seems then to feel a desire to take a turn to the right; checks this desire at first by bending a little further to the left; but then the urge to change its direction becomes irresistible.

The curves of this new style are plant-like, exciting, sensually highly strung and, like everything highly strung, of short duration. This epoch was short; it lasted barely twenty years, from 1890 to 1905. In England it was called the 'New Style', and in France 'Art Nouveau', which is now the internationally recognized name. It was also called 'Cloisonnisme' in France, a name invented in Pont-Aven *Cloison* means partition, and the artists of Pont-Aven had drawn a dividing line between themselves and the

Sketch for a studio-house in Darmstadt (1899)

Perversity, which perhaps accounts for the fact that the bourgeoisie of the great cities accepted it only with reservations, as a form of decoration. Very many artists, especially the most highly individual, were considered degenerate.

The architectural examples are not numerous, a consequence of the short flowering period. There are some theatre foyers, for example that of the Munich Schauspielhaus, some staircases, some garden gates. There must have been many façades; those few which remain have been spoilt by renovation. One of the most original façades, that of the photographic studio 'Elvira' (1898) in Munich was destroyed in 1936 by the builders of the Hitler period. The most remarkable examples of Art Nouveau architecture are to be seen in Barcelona. They are the works of a master who began to build in historic Gothic forms, but who, towards the middle of his life examined the basic structural principles and so discovered forms whose influence extended far beyond the Art Nouveau period and into the most recent times. This man was Antonio Gaudí (1852–1926).

Gaudí was thirty-one years old when he took over the project for a neo-Gothic church in a suburb of Barcelona. He worked on this building until his death, which was hastened by his failing to notice an approaching tramcar, being sunk in thought at the time.

traditional. Another expression, 'Secession', which was coined in Vienna in 1897, illustrates the same attitude by artists.

The main documents of the Art Nouveau are found in painting, in book-illustration and in applied arts. The style arose from a variety of motives: a protest against plush and stucco, nature-enthusiasm, a naïve sensuality at times rather sultry, and a pinch of High-Life-

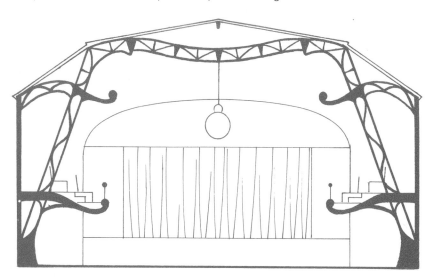

Iron hall-construction for a theatre in Brussels, built by Viktor Horta 1897

The church of Templo Expiatorio de la Sagrada
Familia is a fragment, a four-towered building with a
main portal, turned towards the east, with a wall on
the north side which, in part, is carried up to such a
height that an idea can be gained of the gigantic
dimensions of the planned nave. The plan and the
silhouette of the building are Gothic; but the details
are liberated to such an extent from the traditional
Historicism that quite new non-Gothic constructional ideas are evident. The pointed arches, whose
curves are after all only a part of a circle, are replaced
by hyperbolas, parabolas, curves running into
infinity and whose branches stretch out persistently
until they become straight lines. In comparison with
a circular arch which passes into the straight, these
curves are unbroken and of greater span.

Behind these new arch-shapes are new constructional ideas, which Gaudí worked out in a small way
in buildings which he carried out for the Duke Eusebio
Guell. The Guell Park, which was a project for a
garden city to the north of Barcelona, is unfinished,
like the church of the Sagrada Familia. It is the work
of a mathematical dreamer.

The static scheme of a sloping pillar for a wall in the
Guell Park is copied from a sketch from the year 1900.
It might just as well be a detail for the Kennedy
Airport in New York.

In the Guell Park, concealed on seats and balustrades,

Gaudí has placed inscriptions which exemplify in
rough Catalan his pious introspection. They are
dedicated to the Virgin Mary: 'her tender hands' —
'A body of stars' — 'If only you knew her'.

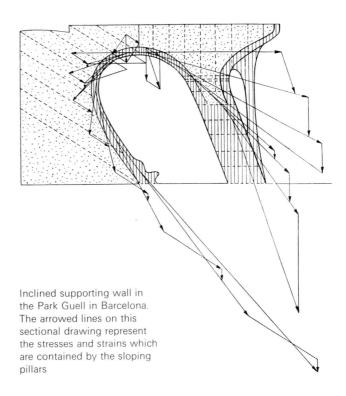

Inclined supporting wall in
the Park Guell in Barcelona.
The arrowed lines on this
sectional drawing represent
the stresses and strains which
are contained by the sloping
pillars

Weissenhof Settlement in Stuttgart, dwelling-house on a slope built by Le Corbusier in 1927

The New Realism

In its initial flowering Art Nouveau began to show signs of developing a philosophy of life, of plumbing spiritual depths. It showed this new attitude in seemingly superficial ways: women began to assume 'secessionist' habits, to discard their inhibitions — and their corsets, to go in for sport, to become more natural and emancipated. Men became more effeminate, unsophisticated, pensive, at times even tearful. Despite this, the style lost its value, at least for some years, and became a matter of fashion. Thus its genuine achievements were forgotten. It became old-fashioned, just as old-fashioned as the former Historicism.

Between the end of Art Nouveau and the rise of the 'New Realism' was the First World War. The old style hung on a little longer as a sort of coffee-house architecture, but it had become so insignificant that it aroused no protest. The only fault that might be found was a backward-looking sentimentality. But this was only a residue, a hankering for the past as an

aversion to unadorned flat surfaces and to the new tendency to display the constructional technicalities which had long been concealed. A building in which you could see the construction seemed naked to the unaccustomed eye. Decoration in the traditional sense had gone. If a cornice were necessary, it would be made as unobtrusive as possible, a sheet-iron ridge, no more. Columns, capitals, friezes, pedestals, ornamentation of walls — all had vanished. The only clothing a house received was a coat of paint at the most a facing of tiles.

Art Nouveau had displaced Historicism and it in turn had disappeared. Nothing of all this remained except a few -isms, and these exhausted their efforts in painting, they did not touch architecture.

Architecture now had new patrons: the industrialists. It is true that in the last decades of the nineteenth century industrial buildings had been erected; but neither the employers nor the architects had any formal or artistic ambitions. Here and there a boiler-

100

house was romantically disguised; there were after all enough cast-iron components with which some kind of an artistic effect could be achieved, but on the whole such curiosities were rare. The great majority of industrial buildings were gloomy, monotonous, formless and, of course, ugly — and nobody took exception to that.

Yet suddenly men arose, with eyes in their heads; men who began to ponder the problems of what would happen if things went on in this way; if this ugliness were to spread out of sheer inertia. In the course of time, so they prophesied, we would be living in an industrial jungle.

Ugly environments bring an ugly state of mind, they can banish all those apparently unimportant trifles which help to lighten the burdens of everyday life. In an ugly environment a feeling of bitterness can arise, and those who are affected by it are not themselves aware of the cause.

The change for the better had already begun before the First World War. The first measures against the rampant threat of the industrial jungle were due to enlightened individuals. Somewhere a manufacturer or a company gave a specialist, a genuine architect, a commission to build a factory — not just of such and such a size, for so many machines, not just practical and cheap and put up as quickly as possible, but with some formal pretensions corresponding to the importance of the undertaking. The building was to be suitable for its purpose, but it was also to be well proportioned, dignified and with a beautiful appearance.

The first buildings to be carried out with such thoughts in mind, such as the AEG turbine factory in Berlin, built by Peter Behrens in 1909, and the Fagus factory in Alfeld, built by Walter Gropius in 1914, did not harmonize with their period, which was still 'Victorian', authoritative, pompous, and not receptive to new ideas.

But after the war these buildings, the first to represent a new attitude towards building, became models. The thoughts behind them were simple, and yet so obvious — looking back upon them — that their rejection at that time seems inconceivable. Let us begin afresh, they seemed to say, not forgetting the

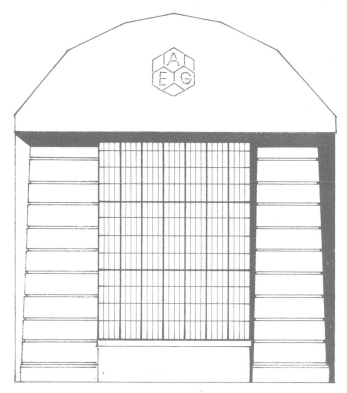

Façade of the AEG turbine factory in Berlin, built by Peter Behrens, 1909

past, but also not considering it sacrosanct and essential of imitation, let us build honestly, without cheating; show your materials and mould your forms according to the materials; plan logically, not ingeniously.

Two organizations participated in the preparation of this new attitude: the Werkbund and the Bauhaus. The German Werkbund was founded in Munich in 1907 by — among others — Hermann Muthesius, Henri van de Velde, Theodor Fisher and Richard Riemerschmid. The aim of the movement was to establish intimate contacts between art, craft and industry; to effect an appreciative understanding between the designer, the planner and the worker on the site; to awaken in the client a feeling for good form and to encourage him to be prepared to throw overboard the ballast which was still considered elegant and prestigious.

101

The sphere of activity of the Werkbund was not principally in architecture, but rather in the requirements of everyday life, such as household utensils and above all in furniture.

Although the target of the Werkbund was to influence was to strengthen the contact between the two opposing camps, to build a friendship between the pure artist and the applied artist (craftsman) and so to rid both camps of many prejudices. The register of names of the teachers is indicative of the standing of

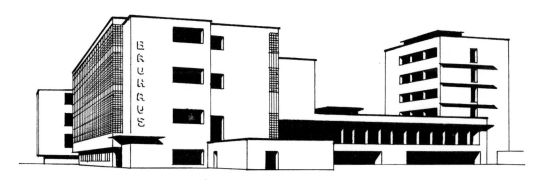

Bauhaus, Dessau. Studios and workshops, built by Walter Gropius, 1925

daily domestic life, although the aim was educative — and successfully so — it was not motivated by any rigid doctrines, and any creed there might have been was so loose and free that it led to no poses or attitudes nor did it in any way restrict the free expression of personality. Following on the pattern of the German Werkbund, an Austrian Werkbund was founded in 1912, followed by one in Switzerland in 1913. Similar tendencies were at work in England, a loose confederation of artists and craftsmen which became known as 'Arts and Crafts'. The German Werkbund was dissolved in 1933. After the Second World War it was re-established in Munich and Dusseldorf.

The Bauhaus was established in Weimar in 1919. Walter Gropius (1883–1969) was at that time director of the Academy of Arts and the School of Applied Arts. He conceived the plan of uniting both schools under the title 'Bauhaus'. The idea of uniting the two

the school: the architects Walter Gropius and Ludwig Mies van der Rohe (born 1886), the painters Lyonel Feiniger (1871–1956), Paul Klee (1879–1940), Wassily Kandinsky (1866–1944), Oskar Schlemmer (1888–1943), the sculptor Ferhard Marcks (1889–1966).

In 1925 the Bauhaus moved to Dessau and took possession of the studios and workshops which Gropius had built to express the ideals of the group. Neither the school, its teachers nor its pupils suited the Nazis with their vulgar and anaemic building tastes. The new power, which now began to establish itself, saw in the school at Dessau an 'un-German' spirit at work, a danger, a breeding-ground for seditious ideas. In 1933 the Bauhaus was closed down; most of the teachers and some of the pupils emigrated.

It seldoms happens in the course of political changes that a new regime arises and forbids a certain method of building. But in this case the course of action adopted was quite logical, for this regime was sufficiently presumptuous to control every form of cultural expression. Anything which did not fit into its ideology was labelled 'degenerate'. The consequences for Germany were depressing. But the general effect on artistic style which had emanated from the Bauhaus in the short course of its existence had already spread throughout the world.

Characteristic of the Bauhaus style is the cubical, the rectangular, the functionally repetitive façade, all words from which a general name to describe the style might be derived. Unfortunately the word 'Cubism', which would not be bad for this purpose, has already been appropriated by the artists. But the word 'modern' satisfies our contemporaries; a word which is of course not permanent, since it travels from one generation to the next; and what the one generation calls 'modern', is no longer so for the next.

Perhaps the name 'Bauhaus style' will be accepted once again, perhaps another name will arise, a name long known, but not before indicative of this style. Another question is, how long such a name will possess validity. The word 'orthogonal' which correctly expressed the Bauhaus style, is no longer expressive of today's work. For something has been added to the repetitive façade, to the cubical, to the rectangular, something which is indicated in the Park at Guell in Barcelona, something which is tried out hesitatingly and covered by a mosaic-like surface: the hyperbola and its neighbour in the geometry of the conic section: the parabola. Both curves, with their arms stretching into infinity are beginning to influence style. In Brasilia, in New York at Kennedy Airport, in the chapel of Notre Dame du Haut near Ronchamp which Le Corbusier built in 1955, on the roofs of sports pavilions, these new curves seem logical, harmonious, fitting into space with geometrical precision. And in a metaphorical sense they fit into a generation of earth satellites, sputniks and moon probes, which prescribe curved courses for their headlong flights.

But whether the kind of building which we call 'modern' will one day be described by one of these geometrical terms is more than we can say.

Notre Dame du Haut near Ronchamp, Alsace, built and furnished by Le Corbusier, 1950–5

103

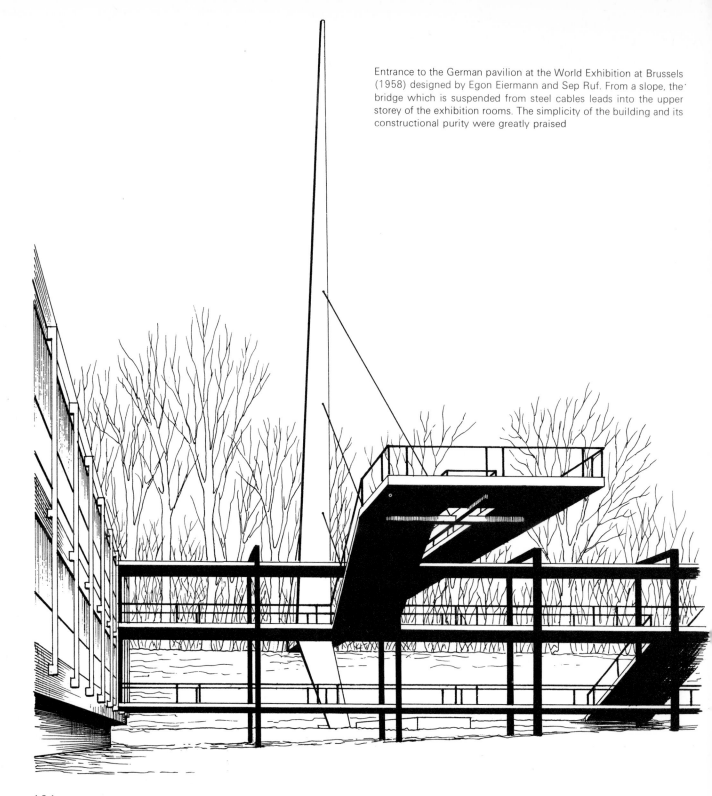

Entrance to the German pavilion at the World Exhibition at Brussels (1958) designed by Egon Eiermann and Sep Ruf. From a slope, the bridge which is suspended from steel cables leads into the upper storey of the exhibition rooms. The simplicity of the building and its constructional purity were greatly praised

The Present

A guessing game might be started about what appropriate name, or what sensible name, might in the future be given to the epoch which we call 'The Present'. As a rule we dodge the question merely by calling it — maybe including the period which we have called 'New Realism' — simply 'The Modern Age'. But this is no flash of insight, merely a makeshift; 'modern' and 'the present' are just words which enclose, as in brackets, a couple of years — at best a couple of decades, which soon hurry on into time.

Anyone who thinks his own epoch to be of special significance will search for as high-sounding a name as 'Gothic' or 'Baroque'. The more sceptical will search for inspiration in dictionaries and textbooks to find a word ending in -ism, which might be pertinent but ugly and will soon cry out to be replaced.

The sceptic will sooner or later give up the search and will say it is the job of the contemporary to help in fashioning his epoch; or if his gifts do not extend thus far, to contemplate the work being done and to praise or criticize it. He need not rack his brains to search for a name. He will respectfully argue that the great epochs were all christened posthumously: the Gothic, which was born in the twelfth century, received its name 700 years later; and in order to find a description for this style, it was necessary to take a word which was already 400 years old and to destroy its accepted meaning.

When an epoch has received a title during its period of existence — such as Rococo, Empire, Art Nouveau, and others — its lease of life has usually been a short one.

A name might be a mere password; it might on the other hand be a word which only in the course of time demonstrates its content and its standing, its origin, its attitudes, intentions, methods and aims.

A comparison with the names of magazines or newspapers will illustrate this point. The name *House and Garden* or *Ladies' Home Journal* requires no explanation. But names like *Forward* are an expression of temperament, not of content. Finally: titles like *Manchester Guardian* or *New York Times* are relatively self-evident. We know what these titles really mean when we have read and are familiar with the written pages.

Our present period has already been dubbed with a number of names, which attempt to be informative: 'Age of synthetics', 'Atomic age', 'Brutalism'. But the suspicion arises that all these names are inadequate. The last is moreover polemical and possibly presumptuous. But it ought to be taken into consideration, for it does express in a contemptuous way our present manner of building.

It becomes obvious that the word 'brutalism' is applicable mainly to buildings which are left in their raw concrete state; also to streets which are well and logically and even beautifully conceived for the solution of traffic problems, but which nevertheless violate the character of a town. On such points there will always be divergence of opinion, and some compromise will have to be sought, since a solution which

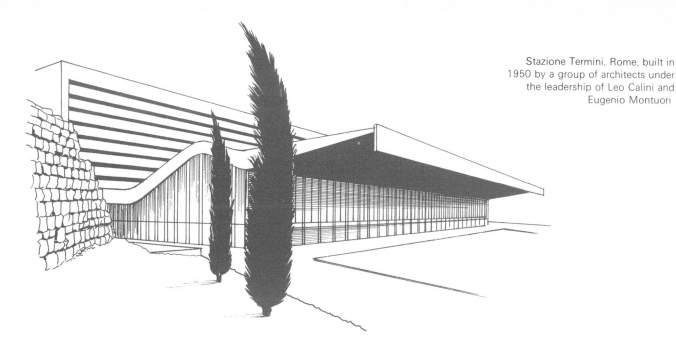

satisfies all parties is probably impossible. It must be said that generally in the past the old has had to be sacrificed for the new, and it was the old which was demolished or mutilated. Two periods: the Renaissance and the Baroque were great not only in construction but in demolition. The Historicism of the nineteenth century, so often abused as barren and pompous, as inferior, did, by its attraction to past styles initiate the idea of the preservation of ancient monuments. Never before had old buildings been restored with such fondness, expense and expertise; and it is very probable that Cologne cathedral would never have been completed without the hankering after things mediaeval which characterized the Romantic period. Today, as in times past, an epoch should not be judged by its negative features, when it also can show a great number of positive virtues.

How are we building now? What are the characteristics of our present-day style, which has not yet been given a name? Is it still in process of formation, is it still feeling its way, or has it already produced works of architecture which will be valid for a long time to come?

The Bauhaus has not been forgotten. Almost everything which was taught, tried out and built in the short space of time between 1920 and 1933 remains valid and is still presentable, although some of its buildings seem now to lack elegance. But the Bauhaus was, after all, only a beginning, and its basic mission — the normalization and the industrial production of building elements — was still in a childhood stage.

Without doubt the Bauhaus is the foundation for today's style: the cubical or rectangular forms, the repeating patterns of façades, all stem from it. To these forms the curve has been added, pleasurable as a contrast to the rectangle, fanciful and inviting to geometric extravagances, which, it must be admitted, sometimes look more pertinent to the construction than they really are, but nevertheless bring some relief to the uniformity of the patterned exterior walls. New techniques have evolved through the increasing necessity to build higher, to build more quickly, and to build rationally with prefabricated units. Much which may seem new is only an extension of older techniques. At the beginning of this book attention was drawn to the origin of cement-work and of walls and vaults cast in moulds. What is new, however, is the perfecting of the material and the technical development of the process. The same is true of skeleton construction. The principle is old: it is seen in the half-timbered house. In such a house, just as

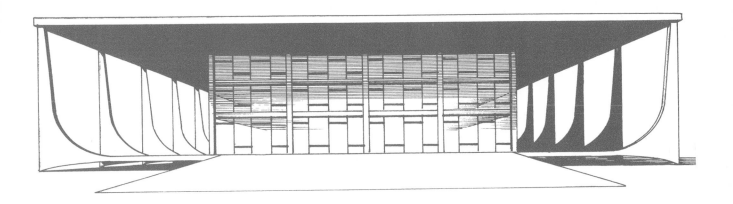

in a steel-skeleton skyscraper, the walls have no supporting function. In place of the old wooden beams, there are now steel supports which arrive prefabricated from the rolling-mill; and for the filling of the walls there is a great selection of different materials which are both sound-proof and heat-regulating. The idea of disburdening the walls arose in the Gothic period and was modified time after time till perfection was reached. Such a process began with technical considerations and out of these there developed the style.

The style of our days is not so consistent, yet it is in many details also the result of technical considerations. The conception of the outer wall of a building as a shell, as an envelope, is a consequence of skeleton construction. The skeleton can be of reinforced concrete, of concrete poured over pre-stressed steel rods, or of iron posts and supports; the walls are inserted. Often there are no outer walls at all in the traditional sense, but only metal frames and glass.

The buildings in which this technique is adopted are light and airy, even when they are sixty and more storeys high.

It is possible to shift the supports of such a house, the spinal column which supports everything, into the interior, so to conceal the skeleton behind glass and interior walls. 'Curtain-wall' is the name given to this building principle which was developed in the United States. The 'hanging wall' is a frame element of iron or light metal, prefabricated, glazed, disguised, which is raised by a crane and suspended from the concrete roof.

Then the façade becomes a reticular pattern, a framework, seemingly too thin, delicate, glassy; able in daylight to mirror sky and clouds or at night to tell of the activity going on within through its hundred brightly lit windows. Later the lights go out one by one. The silhouette against the night sky is cubical. The lower storeys of the façade then reflect the lights of the street, while the upper regions have become a field for advertisements which have nothing to do with the house, and its day-time function; they might inform you that happiness is to be had by drinking a cola or beer; they might write a registered trade-name in blazing light across the night sky.

There are people who rave about the romance of the skyscraper and of the great city, and who say 'yes' to everything. In it they recognize the style of their own times, and they are not troubled by the fact that this style has no name. They just call it 'modern' Expansively the façades tower over the swarming streets, reassuring in their slickness; certainly sober — but orderly, honest, clear — more orderly and more cheerful than the present times which they represent.

There are people who, in their too great respect for old stones, find all this bleak, monotonous, mechanical — ultimately soulless. Moreover, it is not only the buildings themselves to which they take exception. They say, it is shocking to find the same style everywhere, in as far as climatic conditions do not prescribe a few variants of the international pattern. A high building designed and built in Stockholm or Milan, so they say, might just as well be in San Francisco. Modern churches are interchangeable; and as far as weekend houses are concerned, the so-called bungalow and ranch styles reign supreme far and wide; no matter if this type of house is a little too southern for northern climates and has too many windows for warmer climates.

Often there is some superficial truth in all this; yet it is also a positive manifestation of the times in which we live. For if, in any country, an architect finds a new variant for the solution of an architectural problem, one which is exemplary, it soon becomes known to the whole world through the professional publica-

tions, stimulates others, is imitated and undergoes perhaps further variations. A further fact is that a master whose fame spreads can extend the frontiers of his influence almost without limit if he enjoys travelling.

Le Corbusier has erected buildings in France, India and the United States; Japanese architects have erected buildings in America; Oscar Niemeyer, the Brazilian architect, has built a skyscraper in Berlin. Examples could be multiplied endlessly in this international age: Walter Gropius, Ludwig Mies van der Rohe, Richard Neutra, Pier Luigi Nervi, Alvar Aalto, and Eero Saarinen have all built in at least two continents.

This accessibility, this exchange across frontiers and oceans, ought to be considered as a good sign of the times: the decision to adopt a universal form-language in which there is nevertheless sufficient scope for the expression of individuality. Stimulus comes from all sides and is adopted on all sides in a form considered suitable.

Japanese ideas spread throughout California and from then their influence spreads further; Swedish ideas find their way south; and west; Russia has changed its mind and taken a look round the world;

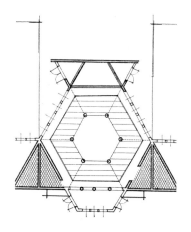

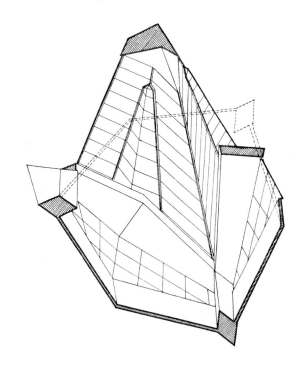

Frank Lloyd Wright 1955
(left) Ground-plan for a synagogue (right) Design for a mortuary. Both buildings are planned as central buildings over three radiating main axes

108

so in future no collective group of architects will hit upon the idea of designing a university with the contours of a cathedral.

If the peoples of the world co-operate in building, this is surely of great promise; it is further only natural, since the problems are one and the same in every country; growing traffic density, growing populations, and the need to rationalize by pre-fabrication.

The sceptics scent dangers, disquiet overcomes them at the thought that soon everything will be the same everywhere. Perhaps the same disquiet caused at first some, and then many, architects who became tired of building in right angles and with ruled lines, to rediscover the curve, the modelled swung line, which had perhaps not received due recognition in the period of reticulated buildings.

The fact that so much, although not everything, could be done with reinforced concrete was stimulating to the imagination, even if it sometimes caused its users to indulge in eccentric extravagances, and thus there arose a new Expressionism which permeated the good old 'New Realism'. A work of architecture should portray something special, a personal stamp, an individual character, nothing at all prefabricated, and as few right angles as possible. After a period of building in sparse forms, after a period of intentional personal anonymity, the pendulum has swung rather too radically away from the orthogonal and the familiar and towards the opposite extreme: to the egg-shaped curve and to the free camber. It seems as if a new Mannerism were about to spread, in accordance with which nothing should any longer be straight, no roof should be flat. Inclined pillars, which would have rejoiced the heart of Antonio Gaudí, are becoming fashionable, walls are being bent into curved shapes and roofs look like petrified waves.

The sceptic scents degeneration; he is beset by the uncomfortable thought that soon everything will be twisted and distorted. As usual, two attitudes become apparent: Some say: 'Oh, how beautiful'; others long for a return to the eighteenth century or earlier.

There are critical voices which discern a mistaken direction in the new tendencies. The new style, they

The reception building of Trans World Airlines at Kennedy Airport, New York, built in 1960 by Eero Saarinen

say, has not arisen from constructional needs but has been thought out as an escape from the boredom of realism. But it is as yet too soon to dismiss the new developments out of hand.

Frank Lloyd Wright's Guggenheim Museum in New York, in which the visitor is led willy-nilly past works of art in a certain sequence by a spiral path is, to some, an aberration. Le Corbusier's little church on the hill above Ronchamp, experimental as it may be, is usually more highly regarded.

There will be many experiments, some better than others, and through all these experiments something new will come into being. Whether it will be Architecture, we cannot yet know.

After pregnant words about the pre-conditions for the creation of a masterpiece Goethe wrote: 'Art must go on creating for a long time before it becomes beautiful.' In this sense every experiment is a tentative groping, a step often presumed to be valid in a direction often presumed to be necessary; and only the sum-total of many such steps will reveal the direction of things to come.

And here the sceptic again intervenes. He says, these are not the days to hope for a new style, to expect something original, or to look for a new Classicism. It

109

HABITAT
Project for a dwelling-house settlement composed of pre-fabricated normalized units, which can be combined in 158 variants to produce flats of between two and six rooms. The plan, which is the work of Moshe Safdie, was executed for the World Exhibition in Montreal in 1967

is not the destiny of this age to produce something 'original', that is, something creative. Such is not possible in view of our inheritance from all former ages, which have been excavated, accumulated, collected, classified, catalogued and recognized for their true value. A gigantic museum, filled with treasures, has been built up and charms our view of the past, dazzles and intimidates us, and leaves the artist hopeless when he turns away.

Whether the doubter is right or not one task for our epoch is clear; to maintain, to restore, to conserve, to save all that is threatened with extinction and to do so with all the technical means at our disposal.

It was right to save Abu Simbel from the waters of the new Aswan Dam. The technical means and the knowledge are adequate, and money should be made available. Figures may intimidate, but they may be justified by a comparison: the cost of the work at Abu Simbel was estimated at $40 million. This could be

the cost of waging one day of a war, if the price of war could indeed be expressed in figures.

Finally, the question must remain open: how will our age, which will soon become a part of the past, be judged by another Present? What will be praised, what blamed? The answers might be melancholy or just resigned. The author would be pleased if his readers thought otherwise. For how should the sceptic know that technology and too much concentration on the history of art and of civilization will lame the creative impulses, as is said. And even if such should be the case for a period of time, how can he know that it will always remain so?

Golden ages alternate with periods of transition and with periods of wandering in the wilderness. But doubts, and especially doubts about the rightness of traditional practice, of practice which is all too often mechanically accepted without a moment's thought, such doubts may have blessed consequences.

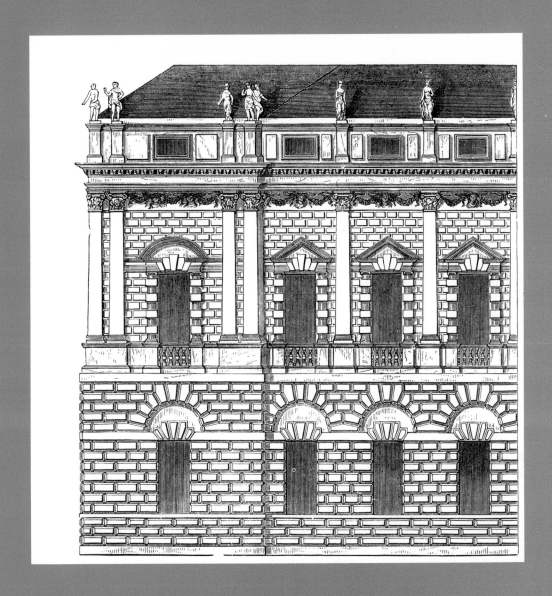

Comparative Styles

(above) Egyptian columns
stylized from plant subjects

(below) Cretan columns from
the palace of Knossos

PRE-CLASSICAL COLUMNS

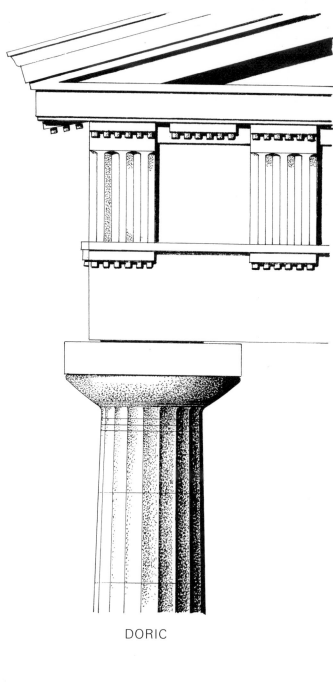

DORIC

THE THREE CLASSIC<

Columns and Entablatures

IONIC

CORINTHIAN

RDERS ACCORDING TO VITRUVIUS POLLIO

Capitals

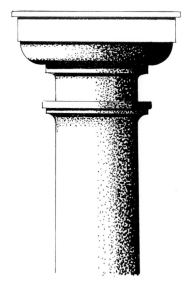

ETRUSCAN
Temple at Volpi

ROMAN
Composite capital

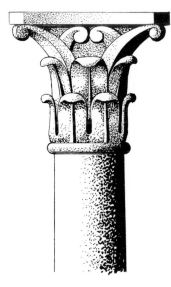

ROMAN
Temple on the Capitol,
c. A.D. 180

ROMANESQUE
Wimpfen am Berg, 1200

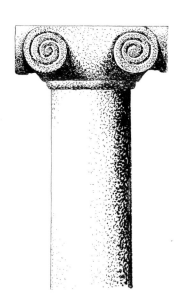

ROMANESQUE
Fulda, 820

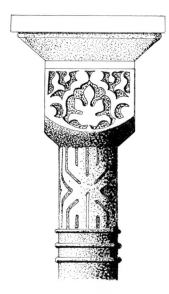

MOORISH
Alhambra, Granada

BYZANTINE
Santa Sophia

BYZANTINE
Ravenna

ROMANESQUE
Cubiform capital

GOTHIC
Foliage capital

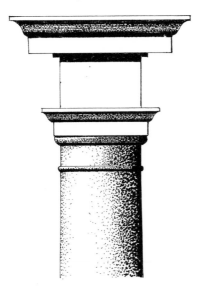

RENAISSANCE
Palazzo Balbi, Genoa

BAROQUE
Volute capital

Pillars

ROMAN

ROMANESQUE

GOTHIC

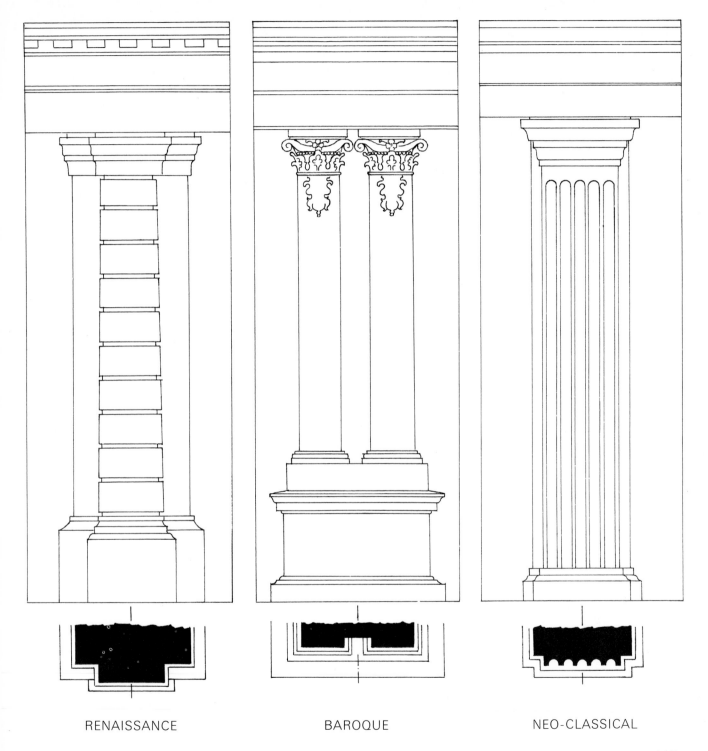

RENAISSANCE   BAROQUE   NEO-CLASSICAL

117

Portals

EGYPTIAN

MYCENAEAN

GREEK

MOORISH

GOTHIC

RENAISSANCE

ROMAN

CAROLINGIAN

ROMANESQUE

BAROQUE

ROCOCO

NEO-CLASSICAL

119

Windows

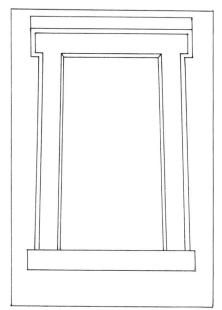

GREEK

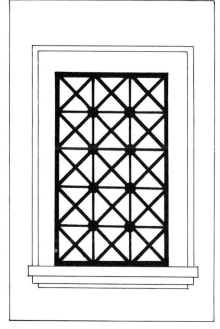

ROMAN

ROMANESQUE

RENAISSANCE

RENAISSANCE

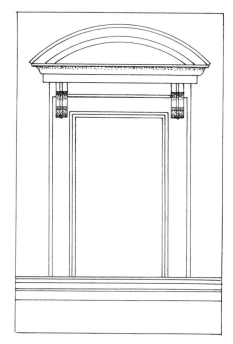

RENAISSANCE

MOORISH

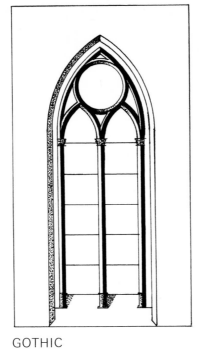

GOTHIC

Early, middle and late Gothic tracery

BAROQUE

ROCOCO

NEO-CLASSICAL

Gables 1

GREEK

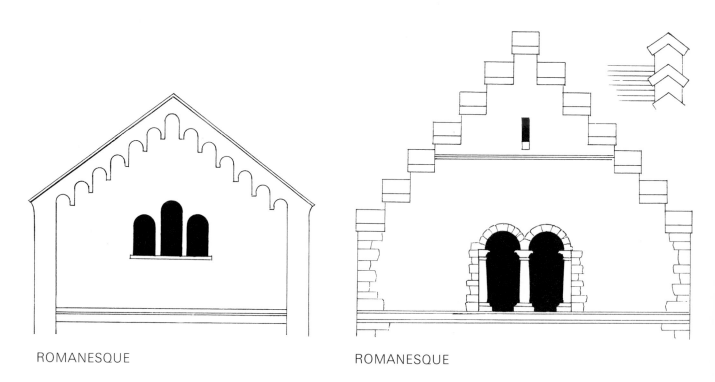

ROMANESQUE

ROMANESQUE

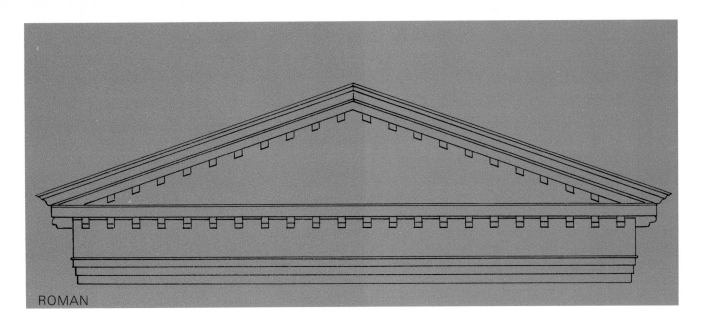

ROMAN

GOTHIC

GOTHIC

Gables 2

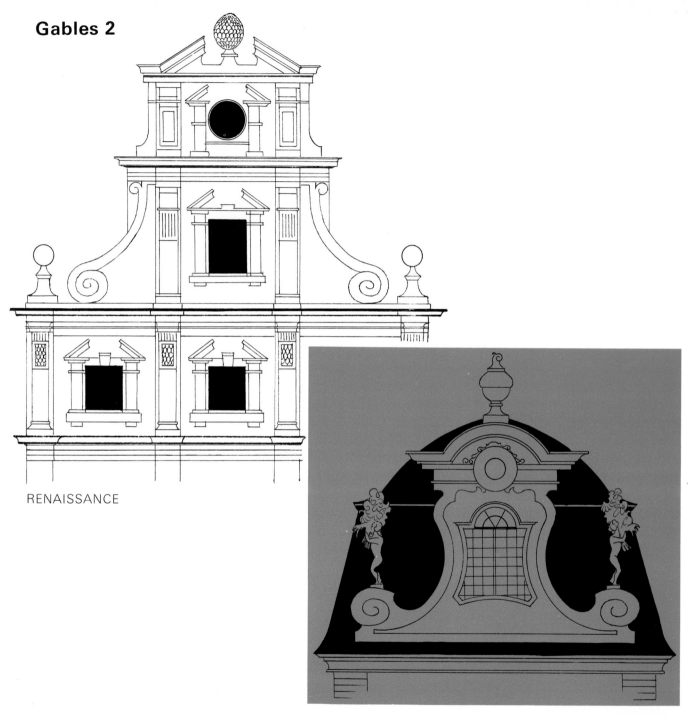

RENAISSANCE

BAROQUE

124

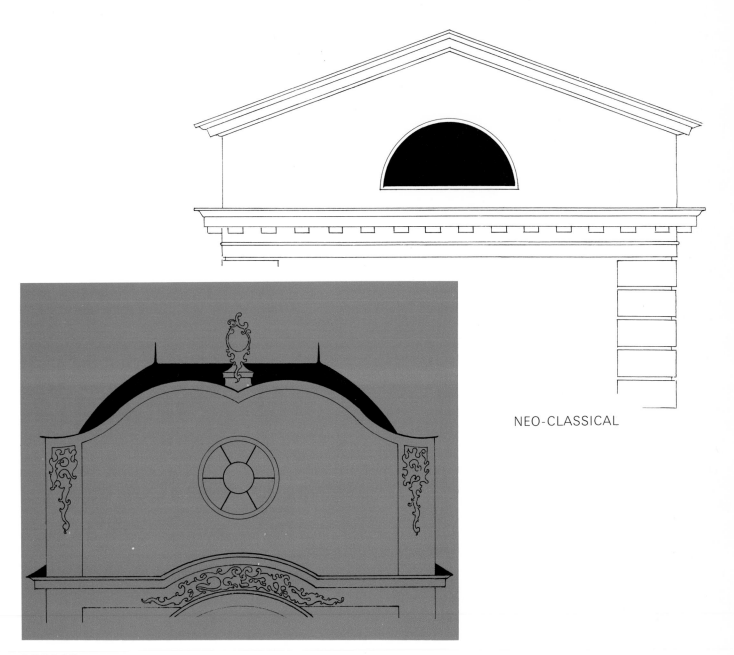

NEO-CLASSICAL

ROCOCO

125

Towers 1

Early forms of Oriental tower
(above) Ziggurat (Babylon)
(below left) Spiral tower
(below right) Defence tower with battlements

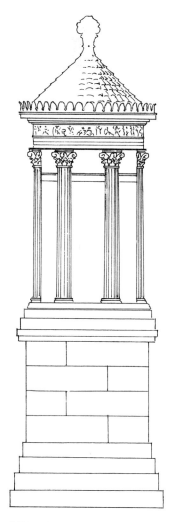

GREEK
Modified round temple

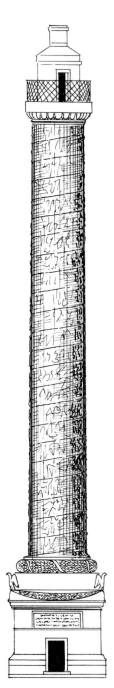

ROMAN
Unique form

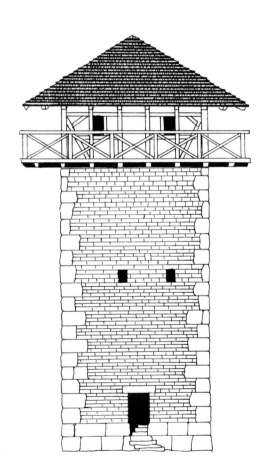

ROMAN
Watch-tower with
wooden superstructure

FRANKISH
Frankenturm, Trier, *c.* 500

SAXON
Earl's Barton, England, *c.* 1000

Towers 2

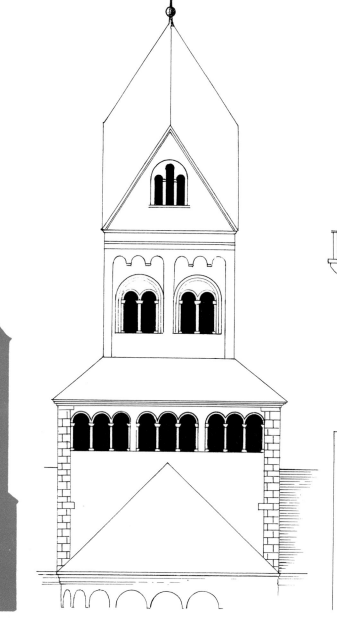

ROMANESQUE
Small bell tower

'Crossing tower' (Maria Laach)

ISLAMIC
(Tower in Jerusalem)

Minaret

Section through battlement

Slit for pouring boiling water or oil on to attackers

GOTHIC
Defence tower with battlements

GOTHIC
Teyn church, Prague

GOTHIC
Esslingen

129

Towers 3

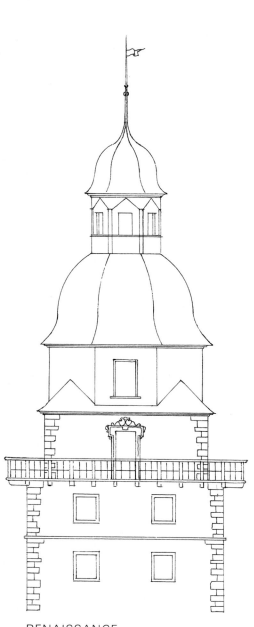

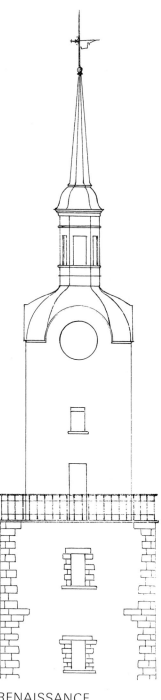

RENAISSANCE

RENAISSANCE

BAROQUE   BAROQUE   NEO-CLASSICAL

131

Façades 1

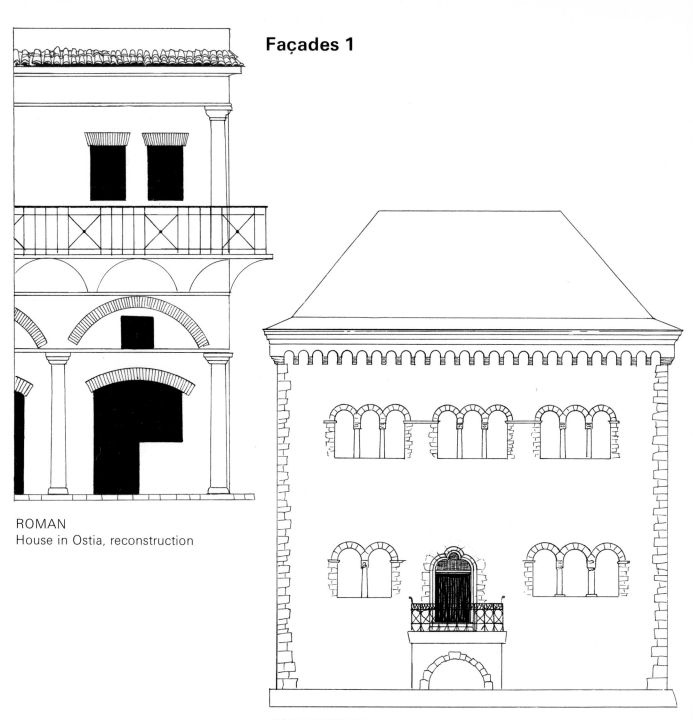

ROMAN
House in Ostia, reconstruction

ROMANESQUE
Gelnhausen, Old Town Hall

GOTHIC
Greifswald, Town Hall

GOTHIC
Nuremberg, Nassau House

133

Façades 2

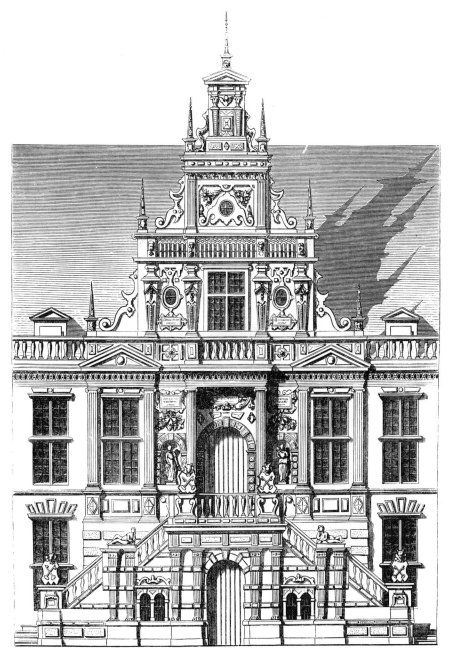

RENAISSANCE
Town Hall in Leyden, 1599

BAROQUE
House in Brussels, 1680

134

BAROQUE
Garden front of the palace at Würzburg

Theatres

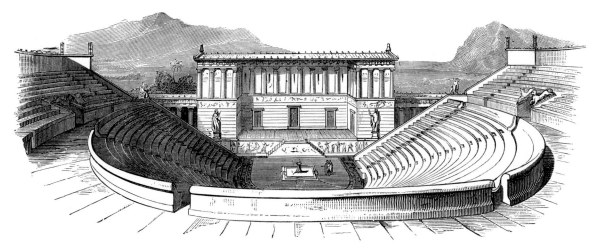

Reconstruction of the theatre at Segesta, Sicily

Ground-plan of a Greek theatre

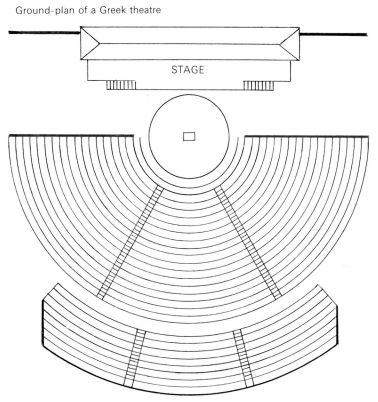

STAGE

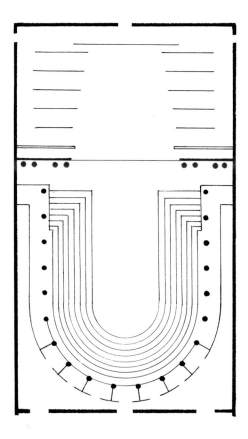

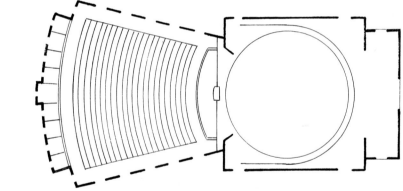

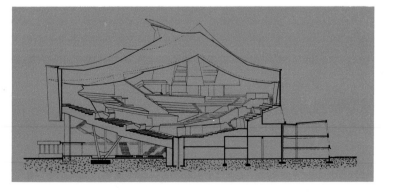

(facing page, right) Ground-plan of a Renaissance
theatre with curtain stage

(top left) The Swan Theatre in London in
Shakespeare's time

(top right) The stage of the old opera house of the
prince electors in Munich, c. 1690

(middle) Ground-plan of a modern theatre with
revolving stage and tiered auditorium

(bottom) Sectional drawing of the concert hall of
the Berlin Philharmonic, built by Hans Scharoun,
1963

Church Ground-Plans

Ground-plan of an early Christian basilica, with three aisles and a small apse

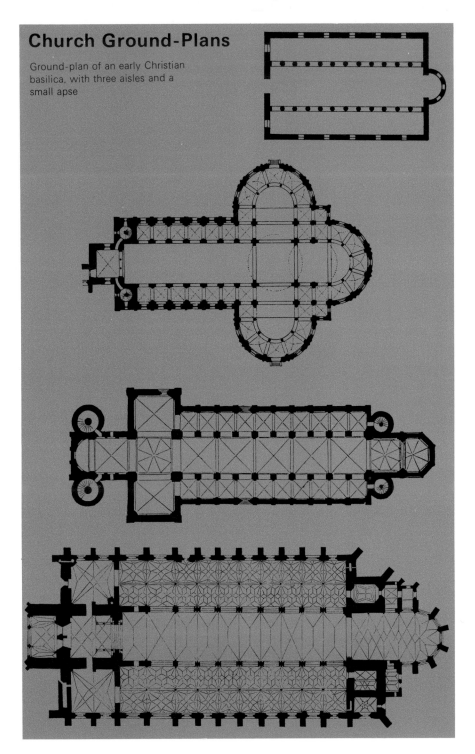

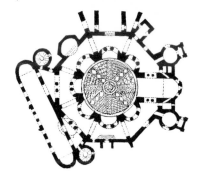

BYZANTINE

Octagonal central building with protruding transverse portico. Ravenna, S. Vitale, completed in 547

ROMANESQUE

Church with three conches (apses expanded to equal the width of nave and aisles). St Maria in the Capitol, Cologne, consecrated in 1067, vaulting *c.* 1200

ROMANESQUE

Building with nave and two aisles, two choirs, four round towers and an octagonal tower over the crossing. Worms cathedral, begun in the eleventh century, east choir dedicated in 1181, nave and aisles completed in 1220

GOTHIC

Five-aisled church with a tower over the western crossing. Ulm Minster, architects: the Parler family, 1377; Ulrich von Ensingen, 1392; Matthew Böblinger, fifteenth century

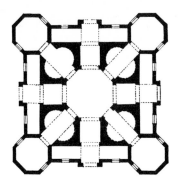

RENAISSANCE

(top left) Church plan by Antonio
Filarete, 1460, for the imaginary
town of Zagalia. Octagonal central
building with symmetrical side
chapels and passages
(top right) Mantua, S. Andrea,
built by Leon Battista Alberti, 1470.
Nave with side chapels and dome
over the crossing
(middle) Venice, Il Redentore,
built by Andrea Palladio, 1577

BAROQUE

(below left) Church of St Laurenz
at Gabel, Bohemia, built by Lukas
von Hildebrandt, 1710
(below right) Paris, St Louis des
Invalides, built by J. Hardouin-
Mansart, 1706. Ground-plan
adopted from St Peter's in Rome

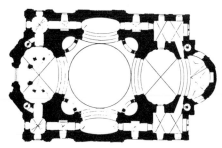

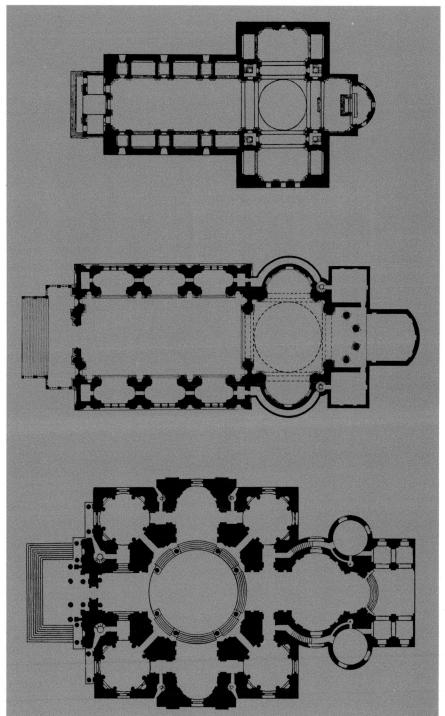

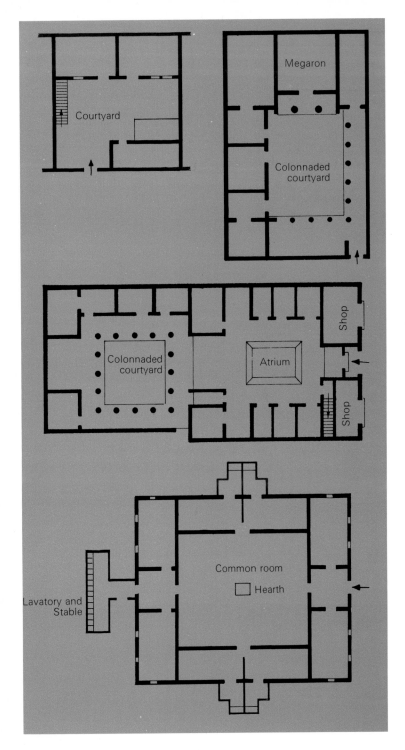

Ground-Plans

(top left)

EGYPTIAN
Terrace house with inner courtyard. The rear portion of the house has an upper storey

(top right)

GREEK
Dwelling-house with megaron and colonnaded courtyard. One storey, with no windows in the outer walls

ROMAN
Dwelling-house with atrium, and behind this a colonnaded courtyard. To right and left of the entrance are two shops, only accessible from the street. There is an upper storey on the street façade

PRE-ROMANESQUE
Hostel for distinguished guests in the monastery of St Gallen. A wooden house on a stone foundation with a central hearth in the common-room and a smoke-hole in the roof, c. 700

ROMANESQUE
Stone dwelling-house, two storeys, c. 1000

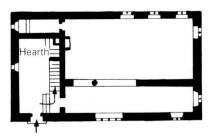

Dwelling Houses

GOTHIC

Dwelling-house with external staircase turret

RENAISSANCE

Villa in Rome with central hall approached via a loggia. Staircases did not become a display feature until the late Renaissance

BAROQUE

Country residence with reception room and conservatory

NINETEENTH CENTURY

(bottom left) Multi-storeyed house, *c.* 1880, with only three rooms facing the street. The remaining rooms overlook a light well
(bottom right) Middle-class house with vestibule. Usually two storeys, *c.* 1810

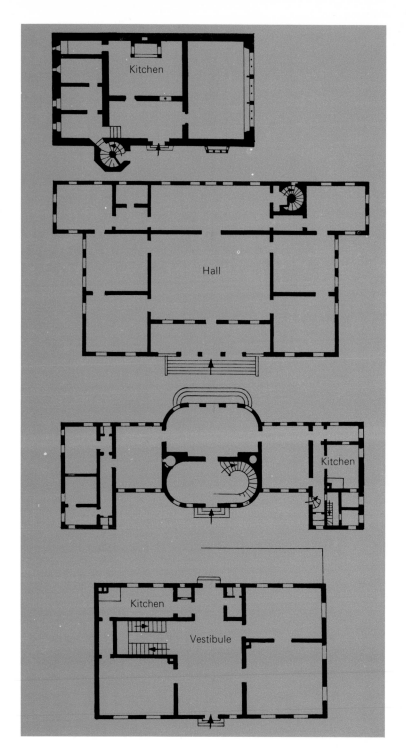

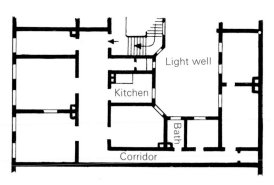

Glossary

Technical terms and great architects

Abacus
Latin, the slab over a capital, usually square and flat.

Abutment
The terminal slab above a pillar or a column, usually a projecting support for the arch.

Acanthus
A decorative element stylized from the leaf of a thistle, essential part of the Corinthian capital.

Adam, Robert (1728–1792)
English architect of the neo-Classical period. Main works: houses and palaces in and around London. Syon House in Middlesex (1770).

Aedicula
Latin: a little house. A niche in the wall for the erection of a bust or a statue, often adorned with a pediment and pillars or half-columns.

Aisle
Part of the church running parallel to the nave and separated from it by columns or pillars.

Alcove
Also 'look-out'. A small projecting extension of the outer wall, often several storeys high, always furnished with windows, and usually a decorative element emphasizing a façade or the corner of a façade.

Ambo
Low pulpit with lectern in the early Christian basilica.

Anta
Projecting pillar; projecting façade of a house-wall.

Ante-temple
Small temple with four walls and an ante-room in the form of a loggia. Early Greek temple-form.

Antefixa
Projecting tile, ornamental finish to the eaves moulding of a temple roof.

Apse
Also called concha, exedra or tribune. The end, usually semicircular, of the choir of a church.

Aqueduct
Latin *aquaeductus*, water-conduit usually in the form of an arched bridge with a gutter on top.

Arabesque
Arabic decorative element; stylized interlaced leaves and branches, used as a frieze and also to fill in spaces.

Arcade
From Latin *arcus*, an arch. A row of arches on pillars or columns; a colonnade.

Arcaded arch
The arch of a vault running into a wall and which is embedded in the wall.

Archaic
Greek primaeval, antique; term used to denote the early period of a style, characterized by severity and clarity of the formal display elements.

Archaistic
Imitating the archaic.

Archaeology
The study of antiquity, investigation of ancient works of art and architecture.

Arch forms
A = round arch; B = pointed arch; C = flat or half-arch; D = horse-shoe arch; E = ogee arch; F = basket arch; G = clover-leaf arch; H = curtain arch; J = Tudor arch.

Arch frieze
Frieze in the form of a round arch, usually under the roof cornice of Romanesque buildings.

Architecture
The art of building. The Latin word *architectura* is derived from the Greek *architekton*, arch artist.

Architrave
Also 'epistyle', horizontal main beams over the columns.

Artificial stone
A mixture of stone-powder or gravel poured into a mould with a binding agent (lime mortar or cement).

When block has hardened it is often treated by carving, smoothing or polishing.

Asam, Cosmas Damian (1686–1739)
Painter and architect of the south German Baroque. Chief works: monastery church in Weltenburg, Danube; Augustinian collegiate church at Rohr; Johann-Nepomuk church at Munich and his own house next to the church.

Asam, Egid Quirin (1692–1750)
Sculptor, brother and collaborator of Cosmas Damian.

Asclepieion
Shrine of Asclepius the god to whom the sick prayed for cure. The temple was usually erected near a spring, where accommodation, lounges and bathing establishments were also provided.

Atlantes
Named after the Titan Atlas, who bore the heavens on his shoulders. A male figure who supported, or appeared to support, some decorative feature of a façade in architecture.

Atrium
The central space of a Roman dwelling-house, lit by a square opening in the roof. This opening admitted rain-water which was collected in a basin let into the floor.

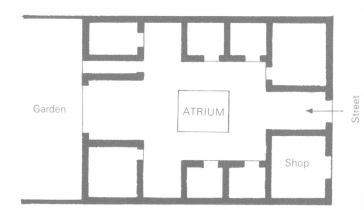

Attic

As a building feature a built-up wall space above the cornice (pediment, entablature) of a building intended to conceal the roof. In the Baroque this was often replaced by a low balustrade.

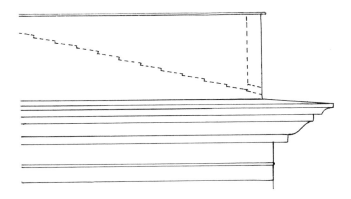

Aula (great hall)

Originally the inner courtyard of a Greek dwelling-house, later a hall, vestibule or council chamber.

Azulejos

Spanish: *azul*, blue. Wall tiles of burnt clay with coloured glazed patterns.

Bahr, George (1666–1738)

Master-builder and architect. Creator of the Frauenkirche (church of Our Lady) in Dresden.

FRAUENKIRCHE
DRESDEN·1722

Baluster

A small bulging column, often bottle-shaped, supporting a parapet. A breastwork consisting of balusters is called a balustrade.

Baptistry

A church for baptism; also a chapel for baptism within a church; sometimes built on or free-standing.

Baroque

For the origin of the word see the chapter 'Baroque'. The stylistic description of the period from about 1600 to about 1750; not only in architecture, but with the same connotation for all the plastic arts and for music and literature, finally for the general way of life of the period.

Barrel-vault

A half-cylindrical vault over an oblong space (see 'Vault').

Barry, Sir Charles (1795–1860)

An outstanding English nineteenth-century architect who designed both in a classical and a Gothic manner. Principal works: the Houses of Parliament (1840–60), the Travellers' Club (1830), the Reform Club (1837) and Cliveden House (1851).

Base

The foot of a column or a pillar, projecting on all four

sides to distribute the pressure on the ground surface. The Doric column has no base; it stands squarely on the ground.

Basilica
Greek: king's hall. In Roman antiquity the term used for an oblong hall, usually with the entrance at one of the narrow ends. The early Christian basilica is a church with several aisles with a high saddle-roof over the nave and lower lean-to roofs over the aisles.

Bauhaus
A school of design founded by Walter Gropius, the Bauhaus flourished, first in Dessau, later in Weimar, from 1919 to 1933. Its influence was international, it extended alike to arts, crafts and architecture, and it successfully aimed at integrating the designer and the machine in a functional purpose.

Behrens, Peter (1868–1940)
Architect, worked in Dusseldorf, Vienna, Berlin. Industrial buildings and dwelling-houses. In 1936 appointed principal of the master-class for architecture at the Prussian Academy of Arts in Berlin.

Belfry
Free-standing bell-tower in towns, often built in the Middle Ages and in the Renaissance.

Bema
Byzantine form of the apse, always semicircular and arch-roofed.

Bernini, Gianlorenzo (1598–1680)
Architect and sculptor of the Italian Baroque. Principal works: colonnade in front of St Peter's in Rome; fountain in the Piazza Navona in Rome; angels on the bridge over the Tiber leading to the mausoleum of the Emperor Hadrian.

Bibiena (Galli di Bibiena)
An Italian family of architects and painters, active during three generations in the seventeenth and eighteenth centuries. Principal works: the court theatre in Mantua (1731); the Jesuit church in Mannheim (1740); the theatre in Bologna (1763); the Margraves' opera house in Bayreuth (1748).

Binder (see 'Masonry')

Blind arcade, blind arch
Decorative use of the arcade form, not passable (see also 'Triforium').

Borromini, Francesco (1599–1667)
Italian Baroque architect who introduced the late Baroque. Principal buildings in Rome: S. Ivo, Sta Agnes, S. Carlo alle quattro Fontane.

Boulle, Andre (1642–1732)
Cabinet-maker and interior decorator of the French Baroque. Created furniture for Louis XIV.

Bramante, Donato d'Angelo (1444–1514)
Architect of the Italian high Renaissance, active in Milan and Rome. Principal works: Sta Maria presso S. Satiro, Milan: new plan for the new St Peter's in Rome; Tempietto in the courtyard of S. Pietro in Montorio, Rome.

Breuer, Marcel (born 1902)
Architect, worked with Gropius at the Bauhaus, first as pupil, then as teacher. Active in Berlin till 1931, then in London, and from 1937 in USA, again with Gropius at Harvard University.

Brunelleschi, Filippo (1377–1446)
Architect and sculptor of the early Renaissance, discoverer of perspective methods of construction. Principal works in Florence: cathedral dome, Foundling Hospital, Pazzi chapel, S. Lorenzo, S. Spirito, Pitti Palace (middle building).

Buttressing
A principle of Gothic construction. A method of support by buttresses and flying buttresses with the purpose of strengthening the walls, which were thin and pierced by very large windows, against the outward thrust of the vaulting.

Byzantine

In the study of style, the tendency of building and decoration in early Christian architecture, characterized by Roman and Oriental stylistic elements.

Cabinet

Originally the designation of a small ante-room, later for a small private or public collection of art works or curios, also for a cupboard of artistic merit furnished with a lock.

Campanile

The Italian word for a free-standing bell-tower.

Canon (Greek: 'standard gauge')

In architecture the repetition of definite dimensions or the regular alternation of definite forms, for instance of façade axes.

Canopy

Ostentatious fabric cover, either flat or tent-like, spread above a throne, pulpit, altar or bed. In architecture, a decorative ceiling of any material.

Capital (capitellum = small head)

The upper part of a column, often richly and characteristically formed. The form is always characteristic of a style or an order (Doric, Ionic, etc.).

Carolingian art

The art of the kingdom of Franconia from 800 until about 950, which owes its existence to Charlemagne. A pre-Romanesque style, stimulated by Italian models. It marked the introduction of stone houses north of the Alps.

Cartouche

A shield or frame-like decoration on a wall, often above windows or archways, often with heraldic significance. usually of stucco or wood, but sometimes painted on the flat surface.

Caryatid

A support for beams in the form of a female figure instead of a column or a pillar. Seldom used in antiquity, the only extant example is the Erechtheum on the Acropolis.

Catacomb

A subterranean burial-ground, developed by the Etruscans in pre-Christian times. During the period of the persecution of Christians in Rome, the catacombs were relatively secure places for meetings and services.

Cathedral

A bishop's church, named after the cathedra or bishop's throne. In early Christian times it stood in the middle of the apse, later to one side in the choir.

Cella

The Latin name for the windowless inner room of the temple, also for the square area of the entire house (Greek: *naos*).

Cell vaulting

A late Gothic vaulting method. The vault is not erected on ribs but composed of shell-formed cells with ridged edges.

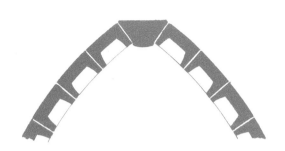

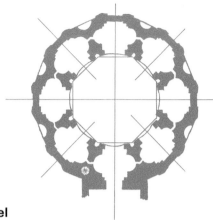

Cement

A powdered building material which is mixed to a cement mortar with sand, gravel and water. Method of production: limestone and clay are mixed, then burnt until they cake; then the so-called clinker is broken; then gypseous stone is added and the mixture is ground. First produced commercially in England in 1825; in Germany in 1850.

Cenotaph (Greek: an empty grave)

Memorial to the dead, often similar in form to a tombstone or an urn.

Central building

The term for a building, whose composition in space proceeds from a central point which is the point of intersection of spatial axes of equal length. The ground-plan is ideally a circle; but it can also be a square or a regular polygon.

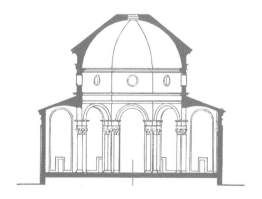

Chapel

Formerly the designation for the prayer-room in a castle or a dwelling-house, now generally used for a small church.

Charnel house

A chapel in a churchyard with a 'bonehouse', in which the bones from re-used graves are preserved.

Chinoiserie

Decorative elements derived from Chinese examples, but subjected to individual and playful transformations: especially frequent in the Rococo.

Chippendale, Thomas (1709–1799)

English furniture-maker, who has given his name to a particular style in furniture, characterized by a mixture of Baroque, Gothic and Chinese elements. Edited an anthology: *The Gentleman and Cabinet Maker's Director* (1754).

Choir (also called tribune)

Name in church architecture for the usually elevated end of the church, containing the main altar often separated from the remainder of the church by choir screens.

Choir screen (rood loft)

A wall or balustrade separating choir from nave in Gothic churches. With lofty mullions, usually with a through passage and often richly decorated with tracery and figures.

Churriguera, Jose (1650–1723)
Creator of a special decorative style in the Spanish Baroque fusing Gothic and Baroque forms. Common in Spanish church architecture about 1700.

Cincture cornice
The main cornice under a roof, the real upper termination of a building, strongly developed in buildings with a flat or slightly sloping roof.

Cinquecento (literally 'five hundred')
Italian name for the sixteenth century.

Classicism
The stylistic tendency derived from Greek and Roman antiquity; not in itself essentially creative, but inventive in its application and transformation of the formal principles which it adopted. (See the chapter 'Classicism' for details.)

Clerestory
A windowed wall in the nave of a basilica above the arcades of columns or pillars.

Cloister
A walk around the courtyard of a monastery, usually developed as an arcade, with sculptured or painted representations of the Bible story; in Romanesque and Gothic monasteries often carried out with much love and great artistic display and with great craftsmanship.

Colonial style
A building style which arose in parts of America where European colonists had settled, using and uniting Renaissance and neo-Classical elements and representing a nostalgic memory of the 'Old World'. The style represents a singular expression of Historicism. Features of Classical stone buildings are repeated in wood, Doric columns are built by ships' carpenters in the form of boat bodies over ribs, Ionic capitals are formed by elaborately turned parts glued together. With all its desire for dignity and display, this style has nevertheless a considerable feeling for domestic comfort. Very many buildings are free imitations of European models.

Colonnade
A columned walk without arches, usually as a passage or gallery, often as the connecting link between two units of a building, sometimes as an independent building. Especially frequent in the Baroque and neo-Classical periods.

Colossal order
A constructional principle for façades, characterized by columns, half-columns or pillars which link several storeys. Often used by Palladio and his imitators.

Columbarium
Storage place for funeral urns in early Christian times, so called because the niches for the urns were let into the wall very close together, beside or above each other on account of space shortage.

Column
A round support bearing the entablature and shaped in correspondence with the style, but also capable of variation within a style and of such importance as a feature that we are accustomed to speaking of orders of columns. (See also the chapter 'Classical Antiquity'.)

Composite capital
A Hellenistic form of the capital, which combines the Corinthian acanthus with Ionic volutes.

Conch (Greek: shell)
A semicircular niche, usually arched over with a cupola. The term is occasionally used for an apse.

Concrete
In its fresh state this building material is a mixture of water, gravel or sand, with cement as the binding agent. When it has hardened, concrete is a so-called conglomerate. There are various techniques: pouring, spraying, shaking or stamping. The final hardened form is determined by a previously prepared mould, usually of wood. Greater stability is achieved through the insertion of an iron trellis as reinforcement.

Confessio
The tomb of a martyr underneath the main altar.

Coptic style
An early Christian mixture of Egyptian, Hellenistic, Syrian and Byzantine elements. The Copts are the Christianized descendants of the ancient Egyptians. Their spiritual centre is Alexandria.

Corbel
A stone projecting from a wall, similar to a balcony head, as support for a cornice or an arch, often also carrying a bust or a figure. Sometimes they are not genuine functional features but are added later as decoration and bear no weight.

Corinthian style
A decorative principle in ancient buildings characterized by rich ornamentation, above all by the acanthus capital. (For details see the chapter 'Classical Antiquity'.) Corinthian decorative forms are especially typical of the Hellenistic period.

Cornice (moulding)
'Bell moulding', cornice or pedestal profile with an S-shaped cross-section.

Cornice (pediment)
The projecting termination of a wall, the horizontal division of a wall, or the termination of a pedestal, a gable, a window-ledge, usually streamlined. A 'false' cornice (pediment) is one which has been added to the wall or the façade afterwards. It is technically unsatisfactory and not durable.

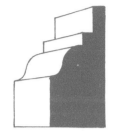

Cosmato work
Mosaics of marble and glass of the twelfth to the fourteenth centuries, named after a guild of artists among whom the Christian name Cosmas occurred very frequently.

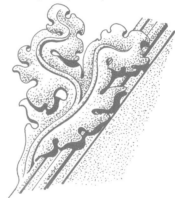

Crab (gable flower)
An embellishment chiselled in stone on corners, gables, pinnacles and tower tops, in the form of a leaf bent and folded; an important stylistic feature of late Gothic.

Cragstone (protruding stone)
A stone protruding from the wall serving the same purpose as a corbel.

Cross
One of the oldest decorative forms with symbolical content. Especially as a symbol of Christianity, the cross has assumed many forms. A = Greek; B = Latin; C = St Andrew's Cross; D = St Anthony's or the Egyptian cross; E = double or Lotharingian cross; F = forked cross; G = Maltese cross; H = crutched cross; J = papal cross; K = cardinal's cross; L = Russian cross.

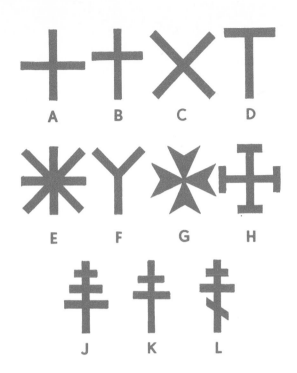

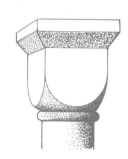

Cross vault
Two vaulting barrels crossing at right angles. In the case of cross-ribbed vaulting, the ribs are constructed first, then the surfaces of the vault.

Crypt
A subterranean burial-place, in the case of churches usually under the choir to which it serves as a cellar foundation. In early Christian times churches were often built over already existing crypts. A spacious crypt is also called an under-church.

Cubiform capital
A Romanesque capital in the form of a cube rounded off towards the shaft of the column.

Cross-arched frieze
A frieze formed by arches intersecting each other; a Norman decorative form (see 'Frieze').

Cross flower
Crab-like termination of a Gothic steeple.

Cross girdle
Girdle-like strengthening of a barrel-vault.

Cupola (dome)
Semicircular or apparently semicircular vaulting above a space. The simplest form is possible over a circular ground-plan. Over a square, spandrels are found at the corners, also called pendentives. (For details see the chapter 'Arch and Cupola'.)

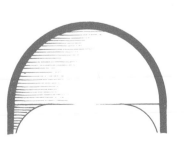

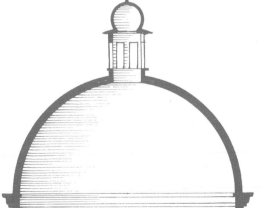

Curtain arch
See 'Arch forms'.

Curtain wall
Modern method of building characterized by walls which have no weight to bear but are added to a previously erected structure (steel skeleton or reinforced concrete).

Cuvillies, François (1695–1768)
Rococo architect at the court of the kings of Bavaria. Creator of magnificent interiors. Principal works in Munich: Residence-Theatre (renewed after the Second World War); the Amalienburg in the Nymphenburg.

Cymatium
A decorative moulding (beading) of stylized leaf forms on the cornice of an ancient temple.

Decorated style
English Gothic period of about 1270 to 1350 characterized by predominance of decorative forms.

Denticulated frieze
See 'Frieze'.

Desornamentado
A tendency of the Spanish Renaissance (under Philip II) towards an intentional avoidance of decoration.

Diamond ashlar
A flat, pyramid-shaped, dressed wall-stone.

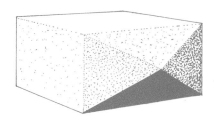

Dietzenhofer
A family of Franconian-Bohemian architects of the Baroque period: Christoph (1655–1722); Johann (d. 1726); Kilian (1689–1751).

Directoire
An epoch of French Classicism named after the Directoire of the Revolution. About 1795–9, but not exactly separable from the preceding period of Louis Seize or the succeeding period known as Empire.

Dog-tooth
A small, slender, three-sided pyramid. An element in the Norman and Romanesque.

Dom
An abbreviation of *domus dei* (house of God) and denotes the seat of a bishop. French: *dome*; Italian: *duomo*.

Donjon
French word for a castle keep.

Donor
One who donates a work of art for the embellishment of a church: an altarpiece, statue of a saint or a window.

Doric style, Doric order
See the chapter 'Classical Antiquity'.

Dormer window
A window in a roof developed as a gabled feature.

Dormitorium
Sleeping chamber, also the house in which the sleeping chamber lies.

Dorsale
A featured wall behind the pews of the choir stalls, often developed as a blind arcade.

Doxale
The usual term in the Baroque for the choir screen,

which separates off the sphere of the superhuman majesty of God (*doxa*).

Drum
The cylindrical body upon which the dome reposes.

Ducento, also 'Dugento' (literally 'two hundred') Italian name for the thirteenth century.

Dwarf gallery
An arcade usually recessed into the outer wall of a church building, high up, without constructive significance, but impressive as a horizontal feature. It is a typical feature of the German Romanesque, but is also found in Italy. As the name implies, it is not passable by pedestrians.

Early English
English early Gothic period, about 1175–1270.

Echinos (lit. hedgehog)
Slightly bulging part of a Doric capital just below the abacus.

Eclecticism
Manneristic selection from the stylistic elements of a bygone period.

Effner, Joseph (1687–1745)
Architect at the court of the elector of Bavaria. Principal works in Munich: wing-pavilions of the palace of Nymphenburg; Preysing palace; enlargement of the palace at Schleissheim.

Eiermann, Egon (b. 1904)
German architect and designer; built the German pavilion at the Brussels World Exhibition 1958 in collaboration with Sep Ruf.

Eiffel, Gustave (1832–1923)
A pioneer in the architectural use of iron and glass, Eiffel's most famous work is, of course, the Tower in Paris (1887–9) which bears his name.

Elgin Marbles
A collection of sculptures and fragments from the Parthenon; named after Lord Elgin, ambassador in Athens, who bought these works of art from the Turks and transferred them to London.

Elizabethan
The last English Gothic period, transition to the Renaissance, named after Queen Elizabeth I; the age of Shakespeare.

Emblem
A symbolical ornament not of the same significance as a coat of arms.

Embossed work
Rustic type of roughly hewn wall construction, used in almost all styles to give a romantic and strong effect (see also 'Masonry').

Empire
The French Classicism of the time of the Napoleonic empire (as stylistic period 1800–30), characterized by the restrained use of Hellenistic and Egyptian decorative motifs.

English garden
Park, garden or open space which has the character of a well-tended landscape in contrast to the geometrically designed park of the Baroque.

von Ensingen, Ulrich (died 1419)
Gothic cathedral architect, worked in Strasbourg (north tower) and in Ulm. After his death his son Matthew took over the direction of the building of Ulm Minster, then his grandson Moritz.

Entasis
The swelling outline of the shaft of a Doric column.

Epistyle
The Greek word for the architrave.

Epitaph
Memorial tablet or stone for the dead, on the inner or outer wall of a church; later became the term for any kind of obituary.

Erdmannsdorf, Friedrich Wilhelm von (1736–1800)
German architect of the Rococo and early neo-Classical periods. Buildings in Anhalt-Dessau, Worlitz palace; interior decoration in the Berlin palace and in Sans Souci.

Erwin, later known as Erwin von Steinbach (d. 1318)
Master of the building guild at Strasbourg from about 1283 until his death. Research has proved that he was not the originator of the plan for Strasbourg Cathedral. But essential changes in the plan are accredited to him, for instance the tracery over the rose-window, which is a characteristic part of the west front.

Estrade
Raised floor in the interior of a room, of one or more steps.

Exedra
A semicircular spacious niche in an arcade of columns; forerunner of the apse.

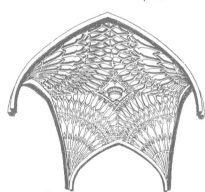

Fan vaulting
Common form of vaulting in late Gothic with the ribs of the vaulting separating out in the form of a fan. Similar to net vaulting.

Faience
Ceramic glazing technique named after the Italian town of Faenza. The coloured, fired glass is covered with a tin (pewter) glaze on which the pattern is first painted with so-called sharp-fire colours. The base is usually whitish.

Festoon
A decorative motif hanging in bow-form comprising leaves, blossoms, fruits and ribbons in stone, stucco; also the same painted on a flat surface.

Figure capitals
An especially frequent form of the capital in French Romanesque, in which a whole legend is often illustrated on the capitals of a row of columns.

Fischer, Johann Michael (1691–1766)
The most important master of south German church Baroque. His buildings are characterized by external simplicity. The interiors are flooded with light and imaginatively planned and decorated. Principal works: the churches of Zwiefalten, Ottobeuren, Berg on the Laim (Munich), Rott on the Inn.

Fischer von Erlach, Johann Bernhard (1656–1723)
Austrian Baroque architect; ennobled as imperial court architect. Principal works in Vienna: Karl-Borromaus church; palace library; Spanish riding-school.

Flamboyant
Attenuated tracery-motif constantly used in French

Ground-plan of the Karlskirche, Vienna

and especially in English late Gothic, to which it gave its name.

Flechtband (lit. plait)
Decorative motif for a frieze or plain surface, first found in the East, developed with many variations in northern Europe.

Fluting
Grooving in the shaft of a column, ridged in the Doric column, with fillets in the Ionic order.

Foliage capital
Imaginative development of the acanthus capital in the Gothic.

Fontana, Carlo (1634–1714)
Roman Baroque architect, pupil of Bernini. Creator of an illustrated work on St Peter's.

Fontana, Domenico (1543–1607)
Architect, above all an engineer. Famous for having transported the obelisk to its present position where it adorns the space in front of St Peter's in Rome.

Fortified church
A church fortified like a castle as refuge for the villagers in case of predatory raids.

Forum
Roman term for the central square of a city in which the market was held and which also served as a place of assembly for political occasions. The presence of temples also gave the forum a religious character. Great cities such as Rome had several fora. The forum is rectangular in shape.

Fresco
Wall-painting using a specific technique. The word derives from the Italian *al fresco* ('fresh') which indicates the technique: the pigment is mixed without a binding agent and applied to the freshly plastered wall, which has not yet set, and which binds the paint when it sets. Frescoes are usually more durable than wall-paintings in which the paint is applied 'dry' (*al secco*).

Frieze
Decorative band – usually horizontal – along a wall or an entablature. This feature may be painted or carved, ornamental or figured. It is usually an essential stylistic feature. A = round-arched frieze (Romanesque); B = cross-arched (Norman and Gothic); C = denticulated; D = zigzag frieze.

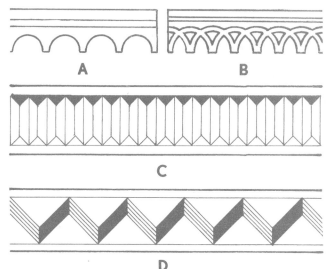

Frontispiece
Pediment (tympanum) over the entrance to a house, also the gable over the projecting middle section of a façade, often adorned with a coat of arms or some other symbolical representation.

Gable
The decorated roofing over a Gothic window embellished with tracery and flanked by pinnacles.

Gallery
Elongated area with a connective function to and between other areas or rooms; distinguished from a mere passage by some elements of architectural distinction. Tiers in halls, churches, auditoria, also in art exhibitions are also called galleries.

Geison
The Greek word for entablature, the cornice under a temple roof.

Geometric
Used in architectural description to indicate stylistic features in which the predominant line-drawing is reminiscent of geometrical figures. Usually the styles of early epochs are geometric; they are usually concise, awkwardly simple, and never constructed with rule and compass.

Gilly, Friedrich (1772–1800)
Architect, worked in Berlin; pupil of Erdmannsdorf and Langhans; teacher of Schinkel. Hardly one of his buildings is preserved. Many of his designs were signposts for neo-Classicism, most especially his design for the National Theatre. To him is due the first restoration and therefore the preservation of the Marienburg.

Girdle arch
A broad-ribbed arch, intended to strengthen a barrel-vault, of both constructive and decorative significance especially in the case of long vault barrels.

Girdle cornice
A cornice which surrounds the building unit like a girdle, usually at the height of storey ceilings or of window-sills.

Gloriette
A pavilion or a small open round temple in a park or on a hill erected as a memorial to an event or a person, and as the name suggests, with no pretension to splendour.

Goldberg, Bertrand (born 1913)
An American architect, pupil first at the Bauhaus, later of Mies van der Rohe in Chicago. Creator of the settlement Marina City in Chicago (two towers of flats, sixty storeys high; spiral car park as far as the twentieth storey).

Golden Section, also Golden Proportion
An especially harmonious proportional ratio which can be expressed mathematically. It can be identified in very many buildings, in the relationship of one component to another, in the organization of façades, and in ornamentation. See the chapter 'Renaissance'.

Gospel side
The north side of the choir, or of the altar, so called because the gospel is read from that side.

Gothic
The great epoch of European art between the middle of the twelfth century and the end of the Middle Ages, extending in many countries into the sixteenth century. For the origin and changes in significance of the word Gothic see the chapter 'Gothic'. The word is used in a figurative sense to indicate a solemnity and delicacy typical of the style.

Gothick
The exaggerated and often ludicrous use of Gothic stylistic elements in buildings, furniture and decoration.

Goujon, Jean (about 1512–1568)
French Renaissance sculptor and architect working in Paris. Principal works: Fountain of the Innocents; façade of the Louvre.

Graffito (also Sgraffito)
A technique for the decorative treatment of an exterior wall. Layers of plaster of various colours are first applied one above the other and then partially scraped off in accordance with a definite pattern. The exposed layers then produce an ornamental form or a pattern of human figures on a background of a different colour.

Nineteenth-century
Gothick decoration

Gropius, Walter (1883–1969)
Architect, founder of the Bauhaus in Weimar (see the chapter 'The New Realism'). Principal works: the Fagus factory in Alfeld; the Bauhaus studios and workshops in Dessau; students' hall of residence in Harvard; porcelain factory in Selb.

Guarini, Guarino (1624–1683)
An Italian architect of the late Baroque. Creator of mathematically ingenious ground-plans; worked in Milan and Turin. Author of *Architettura civile*, a work which provided stimuli in the eighteenth century.

Half-columns
A column of which half is as if let into the wall, not projecting freely, but carried upwards with the wall itself.

Half-timbering
A constructional principle in wooden houses. The walls of a half-timbered house consist of a framework of beams, usually square in cross-section, as the supporting constituent, with a filling of wattle faced with clay. Later brick filling became common.

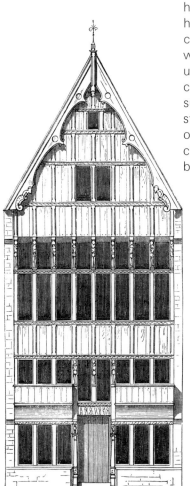

Flemish
half-timbered
house

Frankish
half-timbered
house

Hall-church

A church interior in which, in contrast to the basilica, nave and aisles are of equal height; characteristic of the German brick Gothic. (See the chapter 'Gothic'.)

Hardouin-Mansart, Jules (1646–1708)

Architect under Louis XIV. Characteristic of his influence is the decisive translation to Classicism. The mansard roof is named after him although he was not its originator. Principal works: cathedral of the Invalides in Paris (1706); town planning, Place des Victoires, Place Vendôme.

Helix

A small volute at the top corner of a Corinthian column. The rotation is in the opposite direction to the Ionic volute.

Hellenism

A stylistic epoch of antiquity beginning at the time of Alexander the Great (about 330 B.C.) and continuing into the time of the Roman empire; characterized by a luxuriance of decorative elements, rich friezes, finely detailed capitals, and naturalistic use of the human figure as a decorative feature.

Hildebrandt, Johann Luka von (1668–1745)

An Austrian Baroque architect. Pupil of Carlo Fontana. Worked mostly in Vienna, but also in Franconia. Principal works: the Belvedere and the Kinsky Palaces in Vienna; reconstruction of the Mirabell Palace in Salzburg; adviser at Pommersfelden and Würzburg.

Hip-roof (see 'Roof-forms')

Historicism

A stylistic tendency in the second half of the nineteenth century, predominantly making use of features from past epochs in variant forms; on the whole a façade art distinguished by technical display rather than craftsmanship. (Example: the side façade of the Burg Theatre in Vienna, here illustrated.)

Holl, Elias (1573–1646)

Augsberg's greatest architect. On a study tour in Italy was stimulated by the work of Palladio, but did not adopt the latter's principle of colossal orders. Principal works in Augsburg: Zeughaus (armoury) and Town Hall in an unusual compact style.

Hollar, Vaclav (1607–1677)

A copper engraver of Prague, pupil of Merian, worked in Frankfurt, Strasbourg, London. His works give much information about the contemporary appearance of these cities.

House urn

An urn in the form of a little house, in which the ashes of a deceased were preserved; common in mid-Germany and north Germany in the early Iron Age. From these house urns conclusions may be drawn about the nature of the dwelling-houses.

Huguenot manner

A Classical-Baroque style of building dwelling-houses introduced into Germany and Flanders by exiled French architects.

Impluvium

A square water-basin let into the floor of the atrium. It collects the rain-water which enters through the roof opening.

Incrustation

Decoration of flat surfaces through inlaying of coloured stones into stone. The flowering period was in antiquity and in Byzantine art, but it was often used later especially for floors.

Inter-columnar space

The distance between columns measured from the middle of one to the middle of the next.

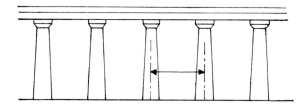

Ionic order

A style in antiquity originating in the Ionian islands characterized by voluted capitals and canalized column shafts. (See the chapter 'Classical Antiquity'.)

Jamb

Receding surround of a door or window opening, in the Gothic often adorned with figures.

Jerusalem cross

161

Jesuit style
A Baroque style of church building in Latin America, distinguished by original decorative features, as these were often executed by craftsmen of native origin.

Jones, Inigo (1573–1652)
An English theatre painter and architect, creator of the English Classical. Studied in France and Italy and influenced by Palladio's works. Principal works: the Queen's House, Greenwich; Whitehall, London (partially destroyed); St Paul's, Covent Garden. Many of his buildings were destroyed in the Great Fire, 1666.

Jugendstil (Art Nouveau)
A style named after the Munich periodical *Jugend*. (See the chapter 'Art Nouveau'.)

Keel arch
In many places the usual word for the Gothic ogee arch.

Keep
Great tower of a castle, often the last refuge during a siege.

Keystone
The cast conical stone at the apex of a ribbed vault. This stone is usually richly carved, often with a monogram, coat of arms or with the badge of the builders' guild. The insertion of this stone was often marked by a small ceremony.

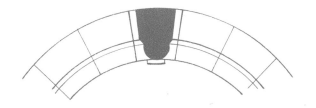

Kiosk
An Oriental garden-house, usually airy with perforated walls, standing free or built on to a house as an arbour.

Klenze, Leo von (1784–1864)
Architect, court architect to Ludwig I of Bavaria. Fundamentally his work is Classical, but many buildings are Romanesque and Byzantine in the spirit of Historicism. Principal works in Munich: the Glyptothek, the Old Pinakothek, the Propylaen, the court church of All Saints; the Valhalla near Regensburg, a hall of fame built in the Doric order.

Knobelsdorf, Georg Wenzeslaus von (1699–1753)
Architect of the Rococo in the period of the Fredericks. Court architect and friend of Frederick the Great. Principal works: rebuilding of Rheinsberg palace; the Berlin Opera House; the palaces of Charlottenburg and Potsdam; Sans Souci at Potsdam. During the building of Sans Souci (1745–7) Knobelsdorf and his king quarrelled, causing a breach.

Knotted column
A rarely occurring form of double column in the Romanesque; the shafts are connected in the middle by a stone knot-ornament. Found in cloisters but also in windows.

Lancet arch
A very slender form of the Gothic pointed arch, occurring especially frequently in English Gothic.

Langhans, Carl Gotthard (1732–1808)
Architect of the early German Classicism. Creator of the Brandenburg Gate in Berlin.

Lantern
The cylindrical termination of a dome, usually furnished with windows and crowned by a small dome which harmonizes in its proportions with the large dome.

Late Rococo
A decorative style at the transition from Rococo to

Classicism, characterized by feeble and fussy adornment, which lacks both the playful quality of the Rococo and the growing clarity of the neo-Classical.

Latrobe, Benjamin H. (1766–1820)
A leader of the Classical Revival in the United States. An hydraulic engineer as well as an architect, Latrobe designed the Hall of Representatives in Washington (1803–17), the Waterworks in Philadelphia (1803) and the Bank of Philadelphia (1798–9).

Le Corbusier, pseudonym of Charles-Edouard Jeanneret (1887–1966)
Architect. Imaginative though doctrinaire representative of cubically clear and functional building, active and influential throughout the world. Principal works: dwelling-house blocks and settlements in Marseilles, Nantes, Berlin, Meaux near Paris; town planning of Chandigarh in India (in building since 1951), pilgrimage church near Ronchamp in the Vosges.

Ledoux, Claude-Nicolas (1736–1806)
Copper engraver, later architect. Precursor and instigator of neo-Classicism; builder of several town palaces in Paris, among others the palace of Prince Montmorency (1769) and a pavilion for Madame Dubarry (1772). His principal work is an industrial plant, the salt works at Chaux, around which he planned an ideal town, which was never built.

Le Nôtre, André (1613–1700)
French garden designer, creator of the Baroque park. Principal work: the park at Versailles, which became a model for numerous other parks.

Leonardo da Vinci (1452–1519)
Painter, sculptor, architect, inventor and investigator; worked in Florence, Milan and Rome and towards the end of his life in France at the court of King Francis I. By virtue of his ideas and his conceptions (monuments, projects for fortifications), he must be considered one of the representative figures of the Renaissance.

Levites' chair
A pew with three seats in which the priest and his two deacons rest during the 'Creed' and the 'Gloria' of the Mass. Often built as a niche into the south wall of the choir.

Lintel
The upper horizontal termination of door and windows.

Loggia
A covered projecting structure of a house on the entrance side.

Log hut
Wooden building consisting of tree trunks laid horizontally one above the other, usually rough-hewn and dovetailed at the house corners. An indigenous form of construction in all well-wooded regions in northern latitudes.

Longhena, Baldassare (1604–1682)
Born in Rome, Longhena worked mainly in Venice. his masterpiece is the church of S. Maria della Salute (1632) and he was also responsible for the two great Venetian palaces of Rezzonico (1660) and Pesaro (1679).

Lotus column
An Egyptian column in the form of a stylized lotus flower.

Louis Quatorze (Louis XIV)
The epoch of the French Baroque between 1650 and 1720. Stately development of architecture under Louis XIV.

Louis Quinze (Louis XV)
French late-Baroque epoch under Louis XV (1723–74), corresponding to the Rococo in Germany and Austria. The term 'Rococo' never gained vogue in France.

Louis Seize (Louis XVI)
The transition to Classicism in France under Louis XVI (1774–92). Restrained in comparison with the

Rococo, often delicately rectilinear, clear and not overloaded.

Lunette
Semicircular space above doors or windows, usually surrounded by a slight beading (moulding) painted or stuccoed.

Maderna, Carlo (1556–1629)
Architect, pupil of Domenico Fontana, worked in Rome. His principal work is the nave and aisles of St Peter's, whose vestibule and façade lead from the Renaissance into the Baroque. Characteristic of Maderna's work is the vividly plastic formation of pediments, pedestals (bases) and all other constructional elements. Other works: S. Susanna, S. Andrea della Valle, Mattei die Giove palace, plan for the Barberini palace.

Majano, Benedetto da (1442–1492)
Architect and sculptor of the Italian early Renaissance, working mainly in Florence. Principal works in Florence: Strozzi palace, altars and pulpits in Santa Croce, Florence; S. Domenico in Siena.

Majolica
Earthenware with coloured patterns, named after the island Majorca. The technique is the same as that of Faience ceramics.

Mandorla
A halo around the figure of a saint, representing supernatural light, elongated, almond-shaped. Not so frequently used in architectural sculpture as in mediaeval book-illustration.

Mannerism
An expression for a style of artistic creation characterized by wilful exaggeration in the representation of the human figure, in the atmosphere, in the effect of light and shade and also in the selection of themes, leading to its own inner laws within a stylistic period of which it usually forms the final elaborated phase: the end of the Renaissance for instance.

Mansard
A space in the roof storey which, owing to the shape of the roof and the windows, is suitable for use as a living-room (see 'Roof forms'). The mansard is named after the French architect Hardouin-Mansart, who often used this form although he did not invent it.

Marble
A gritty crystalline limestone. Because of its colour-tones and its vein-like patterns it has many and varied uses both in architecture and in sculpture. Various epochs have given preference to various colours and patterns: delicate bluish tones in antiquity; variegated patterns in the Baroque for interiors, especially for altars; white in the neo-Classical.

Marble species
Pure white: from Carrara in Italy.
Bluish-white: from the Pentelikon mountains in Greece.
White crystalline: from the island of Paros.
Black (*nero antico*): from the Peloponnese in Greece.
Red (*rosso antico*): from the island of Tenedos.
Yellow and brownish: from Tuscany.
Reddish, veined: from the Untersberg near Salzburg.

Masons' signs
Signatures similar to the symbols of the masons' guilds. They cannot usually be deciphered as they are monograms in code.

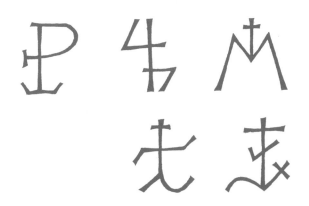

164

Masonry

A = quarried stone wall; B = brick wall with binding and runner courses; C = embossed work wall; D = rustic wall.

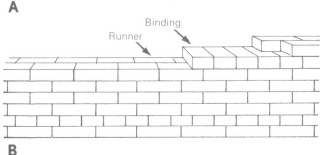

A

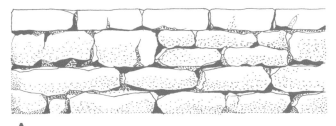

Binding
Runner

B

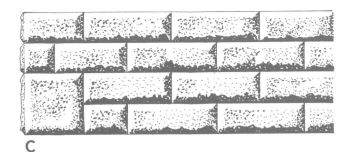

C

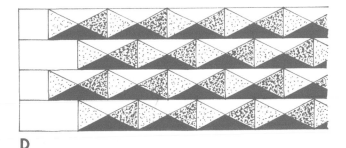

D

Mausoleum

A large tomb. The name is derived from King Mausolos of Caria, who had a gigantic tomb erected for himself during his own lifetime (in the fourth century B.C.) at Halicarnassus. This is one of the 'Seven Wonders of the World': a columned building on a high square base and with a steep, flat-topped pyramid as roof, surmounted by a four-in-hand (*quadriga*) containing the king and queen.

Meander

A hook-formed ornamental strip in the antique, named after the winding course of the river Maiandros in Asia Minor.

Medallion

In architecture a round or oval decoration usually of stucco to fill a blank surface, but also often hanging as an adornment of pillars, sometimes with an effigy.

Medrese

The schoolhouse attached to a mosque.

Megaron

A Greek house form. A rectangular house with a room and a loggia on one of the shorter sides.

Menhir

A Celtic memorial stone; an unhewn, upright block furnished with carved ornamentation and symbolic signs. Prehistoric original of the stele.

Mensa

An old name for the altar in early Christian times.

Men's side

The south side of the church, which in the Middle Ages was reserved for male worshippers; also called the epistle side in contrast to the gospel side.

165

Merian, Matthaus (1593–1650)
A copper engraver of Basle. Significant in architectural and in cultural history for his *Topography*, which he also published himself, containing more than 2,000 plans and views of towns in the seventeenth century.

Metope
A square space in the entablature of a Doric temple embellished with a relief.

Mezzanine
A low storey between two principal storeys, usually between the ground floor and the first floor, but often also between the cornice and the roof; very frequently occurring in the palaces of the Baroque and the neo-Classical periods.

Michelangelo; Michelangelo Buonarroti (1475–1564)
Sculptor, architect, painter, poet; worked in Florence, Bologna and Rome. He is called the 'Father of the Baroque' and all his work is distinguished by harmony and power. Principal works in Florence: David in front of the Palazzo Vecchio, the Medici tombs; in Rome: frescoes in the Sistine chapel, palaces on the Capitol, an ideal plan for St Peter's and a design for the dome. The seated Moses in St Peter's was intended for the tomb of Pope Julius, which was never finished and was later dismantled. Only a few of his buildings were completed under his own supervision, among them the Bibliotheca Laurenziana in Florence and the Roman Capitol.

Michelozzo di Bartolomeo (1396–1472)
A Renaissance sculptor and architect; worked in Florence and Milan. He was Brunelleschi's successor on the building of the cathedral in Florence. Principal works in Florence: the monastery of St Lorenzo, the palace of Medici-Riccardi, the reconstruction of the Palazzo Vecchio.

Mies van der Rohe, Ludwig (born 1886)
A German architect, collaborated with Behrens, Gropius, Le Corbusier. Last principal of the Bauhaus at Dessau before it was closed in 1933. Principal works: German pavilion at the World Exhibition at Barcelona in 1929; buildings in the USA since 1938; Illinois Institute of Technology, Chicago; Seagram building, New York; Lafayette Settlement, Detroit.

Mihrab
A niche; term used for the apse in a mosque which is always orientated towards Mecca.

Mimbar
The pulpit for the preacher in the nave of a mosque (usually made of wood).

Minaret
From the Arabic *manara* (lighthouse), a tower close to the mosque, usually pointed, from which the call to prayer is given five times daily.

Minoan art
Style of the third and second millennia B.C. named after the legendary King Minos of Crete. (See the chapter 'Aegean'.)

Minster
From Latin *monasterium*, the derived term for a large monastery church (collegiate church).

Mirror vault
The ceiling of a room vaulted only round the edges. The central part is flat and is called the mirror. Often used in the Baroque and the Rococo and for the sake of safety usually suspended from ceiling rafters or roof framework.

Module
The semi-diameter of a column. A classical unit of measure for regulating the proportions of other parts (from the Latin *modulus*, a small measure).

Modulor
A mathematical standard devised by the architect Le Corbusier for repetitive units, which obeys the laws of the Golden Section and is related to human proportions.

Monastery

A building complex erected for the monastic life: living quarters, church, farm buildings, garden, usually also library and school. The first rules for the monastic life were formulated by Benedict of Nursia, the founder of the monastery on Monte Cassino (middle Italy) in 529. The authoritative monastic rules for the Frankish kingdom were promulgated on the orders of Charlemagne.

Monopteros

A round temple usually with a cone-shaped roof on columns, a form only rarely found in antiquity but which was adopted in the park architecture of the neo-Classical period.

Mosaic

A very durable technique for the adornment of walls, floors, and vaults, also called 'inlaid work'. Small stones or pieces of glass of variegated colours are pressed into a soft damp base of mortar or cement. The so-called Florentine mosaic consists of very small leaves shaped according to the subject-matter and arranged without joints.

Mosque

An Islamic house of God; originally a courtyard which was in later times covered, usually by a dome. The word mosque (*mazgit*) means 'place of worship'. The Arabs often call their house of God *dschammi*, which signifies place of assembly.

Mozarabic style

A style common in Spain, characterized by Arabic-Moorish decoration on early Romanesque building forms.

Mudejar style

A mixture of Moorish and Gothic stylistic elements, common in Spain in the fourteenth century, characterized by horse-shoe arches, stalactite vaults and richly ornamented majolica tiles.

Mullion

The straight tracery of Gothic windows.

Mycenaean culture

Pre-Classical epoch of Greek culture, called after Mycenae, the most important centre of excavation after Tiryns.

Narthex

A vestibule (portico) at the western end of an early Christian basilica.

Nash, John (1752–1835)

A town-planner as well as an architect, Nash was the leading neo-Classical designer of the English Regency period. Principal works: the Brighton Pavilion (1815–20); All Souls', Langham Place (1822), Regent's Park Terrace (1821–5).

Nave

The principal aisle of a basilica or of a hall-church with several aisles.

Neo-Baroque

An ostentatious building style within the last third of the nineteenth century (the period of Historicism), which might be explained as a reaction against the coolness of neo-Classicism; overloaded with sculptural decoration and with oppressive colouring in the interiors.

Neo-Gothic

A tendency within the period of Historicism aiming at reviving Gothic forms of building and decoration. (Corresponding to neo-Classicism.)

Nering, Johann Arnold (died 1695)

An architect, presumably of Dutch origin, who worked in Berlin under Frederick III. Principal works in Berlin: the Armoury; planning of the district of Friedrichstadt, in which more than 300 dwelling-houses were erected according to his plans.

Nervi, Pier Luigi (1891–)

Primarily an engineer, Nervi's structures in reinforced concrete have been of revolutionary importance. Principal works: Municipal Stadium, Florence (1930–2); Exhibition Hall, Turin (1948–50); Palazzo della Sport, Rome (1956–7).

Net vault
A method of vaulting during the late Gothic period with many net-like ribs crossing each other.

Neumann, Balthasar (?1687–1753)
Engineer, captain of artillery and architect of the German Baroque; equally important as artist and as technologist. Principal works: palace at Würzburg; staircases at the palaces of Bruchsal and of Bruhl; pilgrimage church of Vierzehnheiligen; abbey church at Neresheim.

Neutra, Richard (born 1892)
Austrian architect working in America. Dwelling-houses, industrial buildings, broad-spanned halls. Principal works in Los Angeles: Lovell House 1926; Channel-Heights Settlement 1944. Author of *Biological Building* and *If we wish to go on living*.

Niemeyer, Oscar Soares (born 1908)
A Brazilian architect who consciously rejects traditional forms and adopts a 'manneristic new realism', which is monumental in its own way. His principal work is the unfinished and problematic new capital Brasilia.

Nuns' choir
Not really a choir, but a gallery (choir loft) reserved for the use of nuns attending mass.

Nympheum
In the antique a sanctuary in honour of the nymphs of a spring; later, especially in the Renaissance and Baroque, an impressive fountain or bathing installation without religious significance, usually adorned with mythological figures.

Obelisk (Greek: spit spear)
In ancient Egypt a cult symbol for the sun-god, a lofty stone pillar, square in section, ending in a slender pyramid, from whose shadow the time of day could be read. Later and still today a form of memorial; on a small scale used as decoration for a façade in the Baroque and neo-Classical periods.

Ogee arch
Frequent form of the pointed arch in late Gothic, but also found earlier in Islamic architecture (see 'Arch forms').

Onion-roof
A tower hood in the form of an onion, characteristic of the south German Baroque, often also developed as a double onion. The onion frequently found in Russian architecture is very similar to the German but is not derived from it. In both cases the origin is Oriental.

Oratory
A place of prayer, usually only accessible to priests of a monastic order, later used as a term for the organ loft in church.

Organ-prospect
The arrangement of organ pipes visible from the main part of the church, usually grouped symmetrically and surrounded by decorative motifs.

Ottonian art
The architectural and book decorational art of the Ottonian period in Germany (about 1000).

Ox-eye
A round or oval window, frequently introduced as a blind window in the Baroque for a particular façade effect.

Palladio, Andrea (1508–1580)
Italian architect of the Renaissance, creator of the style later named after him as Palladian Classicism, which is characterized by severe but monumental adoption of Roman building freatures. Principal works in Vicenza: Villa Rotonda, Teatro Olympico, Basilica; in Venice: the churches of Il Redentore, S. Giorgio Maggiore. Palladio wrote: 'Quattro libri dell'architettura'.

Palmette
An ornament whose design is founded on the leaf of the fan-palm; created and widely used in antiquity and used repeatedly in all periods until neo-Classicism.

Papyrus column
An Egyptian column in the form of a papyrus bush.

Parler
An architectural family in the fourteenth century. The name was adopted, for it implies 'speaker, spokesman' and comes from the French *parlier*, which became *polier* in masons' language. The progenitor was Henry of Gmund. His son Peter worked in Bohemia (Carl's bridge and Altstadter tower in Prague, St Barbara church in Kuttenberg). Peter's brother Henry and his five sons worked in Cologne, Ulm, Freiburg, Vienna, Prague, Ratisbon, Gmund, Nuremberg, and other places.

Parler research
A theme in the history of art which is not yet finally resolved concerning the work of the Parler family, of whom eight are known by name. Peter, the most famous, lived from 1330 to 1399 and worked in Prague for Charles IV. One of his sons, Wenzel, became cathedral architect in Vienna in 1400 and went to Milan in 1403 to take charge of the cathedral craftsmen's guild there.

Partition Arch
The arch which carries the partition wall. This wall separates the nave from the aisles in a basilica.

Pass
In the language of the Gothic craftsmen this signifies an arc described with a compass. This explains the naming of the tracery designs: three-pass, four-pass, multiple-pass.

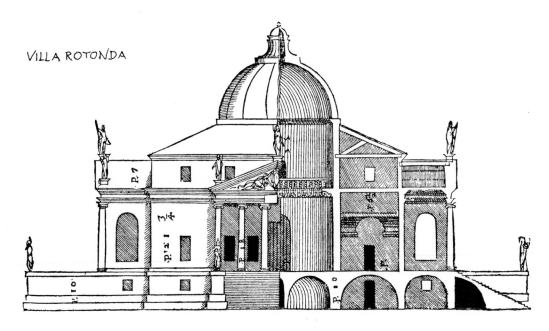

VILLA ROTONDA

Patio
The inner courtyard of a Spanish house.

Pavement
A stone floor, stone paving.

Pavilion
The word derives from the French *papillon* (butterfly), and was originally the term for a square tent. In architectural terminology detached garden-houses are so called, as well as small airy annexes to larger buildings.

Paxton, Sir Joseph (1856–1924)
Originally a gardener, Paxton designed the most revolutionary iron and glass building of Victorian England – the Crystal Palace (1850–1).

Pediment (base)
The lower projecting part of a wall, a pillar or a column.

Pendentive
The spandrel which forms a transition from the round base of a vault to the square foundation.

Pergola
An open arbour (bower) as addition to a building or as a covered walk in a garden. Pillars or columns support a thin framework which is overgrown with climbers (vine, honeysuckle, etc.) which afford shade.

Peripter
A temple with a peristyle surrounding it on all sides.

Peristyle
The columned courtyard of a Greek or a Roman dwelling-house, often given the form of a garden, or as the passage through to the garden.

Perpendicular style
The English late Gothic form from about 1350 until the sixteenth century, characterized by perpendicular

mullions in the very large windows and by fan vaulting.

Perrault, Claude (?1613–1688)
A French architect under Louis XIV. Principal work: the eastern façade (colonnade) of the Louvre, in the planning of which he competed with Bernini.

Pilaster
A pillar projecting from a wall serving to strengthen the wall, but often used purely decoratively.

Pinacotheca (Greek: 'collection of pictures')
In Athens a side-wing of the Propylaea in which votive tablets were preserved. Today it is a term used to denote a picture gallery.

Pinnacle
A slender small decorative tower often found in the Gothic; used wherever possible in late Gothic on buttresses, on the corners of towers and gables, also as decoration in the interior on altars and pulpits.

Piranesi, Giovanni Battista (1720–1778)
Architect and copper engraver working in Rome. Of his few buildings only the church of S. Maria del Priorato remains. His main achievements are illustrative: he designed grandiose architectural representations, *Vedute di Roma* and architectural phantasies, *Carceri d'Invenzione.*

Pisano, Andrea (about 1290–1348)
Sculptor and architect of the Italian Gothic; worked in Orvieto, Pisa and Florence. Principal work: bronzes and marble figures in the cathedral at Florence.

Piscina
A water-basin on the interior wall of a church, as font or for washing the holy vessels.

Pithos
A very tall earthenware vessel (up to two metres) for

the storing of provisions; also used for burying the dead in a crouching position.

Plinth
The base of a column, a pillar or a statue.

Poelzig, Hans (1869–1936)
An architect working in Breslau, Dresden and Berlin. Also a teacher. He was throughout his active life a representative of the 'New Realism'. But he also created works of gracious charm, such as the reconstruction of the Grosses Schauspielhaus (principal theatre) in Berlin. Typical works are the watertower in Posen and the steel-framed building for IG-Farben in Frankfurt.

Pointed arch
A Gothic building form for portals, windows and vaults. (See 'Arch-forms' and the chapter 'Gothic'.)

Polygon
A many-sided figure. In the language of style it usually implies a regular polygon and the building erected over it.

Poppelmann, Mathes Daniel (1662–1736)
Architect at the court of August the Strong in Dresden. He created the so-called Zwinger, a spirited Baroque setting for ostentatious court hospitality.

Portal
The main entrance, which in all epochs was fashioned with special display, representing the typical stylistic features of the period. An elaborate portal standing free without a building behind it is an arch of triumph.

Portico
A projecting structure in front of the entrance of a building usually consisting of a pediment carried on columns. This form arose in antiquity and was later adopted in the Renaissance and in neo-Classicism.

Prandtauer, Jakob (?1658–1726)
An Austrian architect who together with Fischer von Erlach determined the course of church building in Austria. His earlier works have not been preserved. His principal work is the monastery at Melk, built on a great rock outcrop and towering above the Danube.

Profile
In architecture the sectional outline of a cornice, a moulding, a pedestal or a post (support bracket).

Pronaos
The vestibule in front of the body of a temple.

Propylaeum
A columned porch, entrance to the temple precincts.

Prostyle
A temple with an open columned portico as façade.

Protorenaissance
Pre-Renaissance, the term suggested by Jacob Burckhardt for the period at the end of the Gothic in Italy, which can be considered as the transition to the Renaissance. The term itself and the theory attached to it are controversial.

Pseudo-basilica
A hall church with a high nave.

Pulpit
Pew for preaching the sermons. An elevated place in the church, usually against a pillar and surrounded by a balustrade, often also surmounted by a canopy.

Pylon
A towering projecting structure in front of a building; also one standing independently to mark the boundary of a special area.

Quadriga
A four-in-hand. A group of statuary representing a Roman triumphal chariot with the driver in a dominating attitude. The representation may be personal or allegorical.

Quattrocento (Italian 'four hundred')
In Italy and in Italian art the usual term for the fifteenth century; early Renaissance.

Raffaello Santi (1483–1520)
An Italian painter, later also architect working in Rome. After Bramante's death he directed the building of St Peter's (1515). His work as an architect has been greatly overshadowed by his reputation as a painter. Principal works: frescoes in the Vatican, Stanze and the Sistine chapel. Frescoes in the Villa Farnesina in Rome.

Rayonnant
Radiating Gothic tracery, frequent in rose-windows, the great round windows above portals.

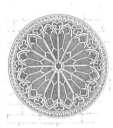

Refectory
The dining-room in a monastery, usually accessible from the cloisters and lying on the side furthest away from the church.

Regency
A short period of French art during the regency of Philip of Orleans (1715–23) characterized by light, elegant construction.

Relief
Sculpture in which the figures protrude flat or half-moulded from the surface. In ancient Egyptian reliefs the figures are cut or chiselled into the surface.

Renaissance
A stylistic term, at the same time the designation for the way of life which developed from Humanism, first called *rinascita* by Vasari in 1550. (For details see the chapter 'Renaissance'.)

Rhythmic travée
The alternation of column and pillar as supports for a barrel-vault.

Rocaille
Shellwork. An ornamental form in the Rococo, of stucco or carving, designed in wave-like, shell-like or snake-like curves, in low relief and usually unsymmetrical.

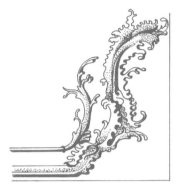

Rococo
The end of the late Baroque period, characterized by the transformation of the too powerful, curvilinear and plastic forms into something elegantly frivolous. Its principal form is the rocaille (rock-work, grotto-work). Shows a preference for the oval and for rooms with the corners rounded off.

Roentgen, David (1743–1807)
A German furniture-maker, creator of a style which was named after him in his own lifetime which lies between the Rococo and neo-Classicism. Roentgen furniture, which was popular in Germany, France and England has slender legs, and is made of costly woods and richly inlaid.

Romanesque
A comprehensive term for all stylistic artistic expression from about the year 1000 into the thirteenth century. Its features are round arches, thick walls, rectangular ground-plans, variety of construction of columns and capitals, decoration of arches. The general mood is tranquil, heavy but not gloomy.

Romantic
The term for the attitude of mind prevalent at the beginning of the nineteenth century, which turned aside from the present and the recent past and

dreamed up a picture of the humane and natural Middle Ages; filled with a love for old tales and folksongs; fanatically devoted to freedom and given to a cheerful melancholy. The Romantic expressed itself first in literature and painting and later in music. It was above all the pioneer of the tendency to preserve and care for old monuments, it assumed the duty of maintaining that which was old in every epoch, and of studying past civilizations.

Roof-forms
A = Lean-to roof; B = gable roof (span roof); C = tent-roof; D = hip-roof; E = deformed hip-roof; F = mansard roof.

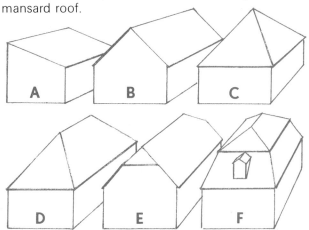

Rose
The large round window over the portal of a Gothic church, constructed with tracery.

Rosette
A circular ornamental form using leaf or wreath decoration, widely used from the earliest times and in all stylistic epochs.

Rotunda
A round building, or the round part of a building, or the circular space under a dome.

Royal gallery
A blind arcade with statues of kings, usually above the main entrance to a Gothic church.

Ruin
A dilapidated building. The attitude towards ruins has changed in the course of time. Ruins served as quarries, but later seemed worthy of preservation and were saved from further decay (even in the Renaissance and still more in the neo-Classical period). In the Romantic period new buildings were erected in the form of ruins.

Runner
A brick or stone in a wall which is laid longitudinally in contrast to the 'binder', which in the case of thick walls binds the longitudinal courses.

Running dog
A strip ornament in the antique in the form of stylized waves, also called 'wave-band'.

Russian style
The particular style of church building which was developed in Russia from the Byzantine and used for Greek-Catholic churches. Features: in the interior the division of the Holy of Holies from the congregation by the iconastasis, a screen of half or full height on which the icons are placed; the use of decorative themes derived from the Oriental; Baroque forms are frequent, above all onion-shaped caps to towers, often richly gilt. Secular buildings of a specifically Russian style are rare. After the eighteenth century the Russian style only survives in the painting of icons. Later architectural stimuli came from Germany, Italy and France.

Rustication
Walls of hewn stone whose fronts are worked geometrically, either roughly or finely.

Saarinen, Eero (1910–1961)
A Finnish architect who worked in America in partnership with his father Eliel. Principal works: industrial buildings; churches; Motors Technical Center, Michigan; TWA Terminal, Kennedy Airport, New York, 1961.

Sacristy (vestry)
A small side-room in a church, usually near the choir, often built on outside and accessible from outside. The sacristy serves as a depository for the sacerdotal vestments and vessels; here the priest enrobes; here also relics and votive gifts are preserved.

St Peter's cross
A Latin cross standing reversed as a memorial to the Martyrdom of St Peter, who was crucified head downwards.

Sandrart, Joachim von (1606–1688)
German painter and illustrator, of great importance for the publication of copper engravings: *Deutsche Akademie der edlen Bau-, Bild-, und Malerkunste* (German academy for the arts of architecture, sculpture and painting) (1679–83), an important source book for research in the history of culture. Sandrart was stimulated to undertake this, his life's work, by the work of Vasari.

Sarcophagus
An impressive coffin, which is displayed openly in the crypt or in the burial-chamber, never buried in the earth. It is usually of stone or bronze and adorned with some display. The dead person is often represented on the lid in a sleeping posture. The Greek word actually signifies 'flesh eater', for the Greeks believed that granite had the quality of consuming the flesh and only leaving the bones.

KISCHI
CHRISTI VERKLÄRUNG

Schinkel, Carl Friedrich (1781–1841)

Architect and painter, the most productive architect of the German neo-Classical period; worked in Berlin; pupil of Gilly. His earlier works are severely classical. In his later works and plans he tended rather towards neo-Byzantine and neo-Gothic. (Details in the chapter 'Classicism'.)

Carl Friedrich Schinkel,
Nikolaikirche, Potsdam

Schlaun, Johann Conrad (1695–1773)

Architect, pupil of Balthasar Neumann, worked principally in Westphalia. Works in Munster: the church of St Clemens and the palace of the prince-bishop.

Schluter, Andreas (?1660–1714)

Sculptor and architect. Less fortunate as an architect, but famous as the creator of grandiose architectural sculpture and monuments. Principal works: sculpture on the Armoury in Berlin, the building of which he continued after the death of Nering (1695). Equestrian statue of the Elector Frederick III.

Scroll-work

Strong curved embellishment which developed in Germany, Flanders and in Holland about the middle of the sixteenth century. The constantly recurring motif is the band rolled inwards. Scroll-work was carved (on door-panelling and furniture), rendered in stucco, also painted plastically to create the illusion of three dimensions.

Segment arch (or half-arch)
See 'Arch-forms'.

Segment window

A semicircular window in mezzanine floors and often used in neo-Classical gables.

Semper, Gottfried (1803–1879)

A German architect of Historicism. Worked at first in Dresden, later in London, Zurich and Vienna. Principal work: the Opera House in Dresden (burnt down in 1869); Semper influenced architectural ideas of his time through the periodical: *Style in the technical arts*.

Serlio, Sebastiano (1475–1554)
An Italian architect working in Bologna and Fontaine-bleau; significant as architect-theoretician and as translator of the works of Vitruvius.

Sgraffito
Scraped plaster-work, a decorative form of wall treatment (see 'Graffito').

Shaft ring
A cornice type of ring running round a cluster of Gothic pillars and seeming to bind them together.

Sheraton, Thomas (1751–1806)
An English furniture-maker. His furniture which is illustrated in technical and textbooks is distinguished by an unpretentious plainness. It is definitely neo-Classical, often with slender legs and has a refinement of surface.

Skidmore, Louis (1897–1962)
An American architect, founder of the planning office SOM (Skidmore, Owings and Merril) with more than a hundred assistants. Principal works: Oakridge in Tennessee, plant for the production of the atom bombs, 1943; Lever Building, New York, 1952.

Soane, Sir John (1753–1837)
A pioneer of the Classical Revival in England. Principal works: the Bank of England (1759–1827); Dulwich Picture Gallery (1812); 13 Lincoln's Inn Fields, London (1809); Tyringham House (1793–6).

Solar
A balcony with open access and masonry balustrade. The term is only used in application to castles.

Soufflot, Jacques-Germain (1713–1780)
A French architect and pioneer of neo-Classicism in France. His principal work: the church of St-Genevieve in Paris which later became the Pantheon. Soufflot travelled much in Italy. He was the first to measure the temple of Paestum.

Spandrel
The space between two arches; or the triangular curved space between the round arch and the rectangular formed by the mouldings enclosing it, which is then called a vault-spandrel.

Spiral tower
A Gothic tower with a spiral staircase in the interior, sometimes half built into the wall of the house.

Spiral tower on a French house

Stair gable
See 'Step gable'.

Stalactite vault
A form of vault developed in Islamic architecture, grotto-like in character. The vault is lined with numerous formations resembling stalactites.

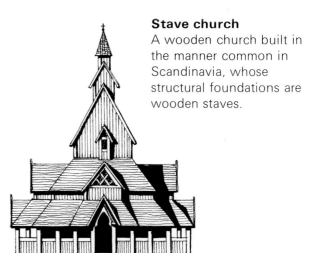

Stave church
A wooden church built in the manner common in Scandinavia, whose structural foundations are wooden staves.

Stele

An erect slab or flat pillar as gravestone, memorial or dedicatory gift. The form comes from antiquity. The earliest steles are of wood.

Step gable

A blind gable graduated step-wise; common in the Dutch and North German Renaissance.

Stoa (Greek: vestibule, lobby)

Stone-chest grave

A tomb composed of stone slabs, common in the Bronze Age in central and eastern Europe; forerunner of the vault and the sarcophagus. The so-called soul-hole in the front slab probably served for the presentation of votive gifts.

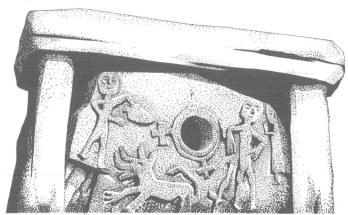

Storoschewaja, Caucasus

Stucco

A form of plastic adornment consisting of a mixture of plaster and water with the addition of lime and sand, which is plastic when freshly mixed. The work requires skill and practice as corrections cannot be made once the material has set. The technique comes from the East, but was already known in Europe in the early Middle Ages. The method is suitable for the representation of human figures as well as for mere ornamentation.

Stucco marble

Coloured stucco used to imitate marble. The marble effect is achieved by allowing the variously coloured stucco elements to run into each other. This technique has the advantage of allowing a free choice of colours. It was often used in the construction of altars in the Baroque period.

Stucco lustro

Stucco applied flat and then smoothed and waxed with a hot trowel, giving it a shiny surface.

Style

The word comes from the Latin *stilus*, an implement for writing (pen). Since the eighteenth century it has been used in its present sense, to embrace all the formal manifestations of a particular epoch.

Stylization

The simplification by geometry of natural forms and models. The clearest examples of stylization are the acanthus and the palmette.

Stylobate

The substructure of an antique temple, usually with three steps. The steps are twice, sometimes three times, the height of ordinary steps.

Support alternation

A principle often applied in mediaeval basilicas by interrupting the uniformity of a row of columns by pillars. Generally one pillar follows two columns: P-C-C-P-C-C-P; but sometimes the formula is P-C-C-C-P-C-C-C-P, etc.

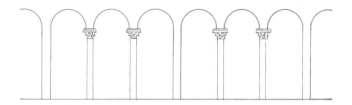

Sullivan, Louis (1856–1924)

Original yet eclectic, Sullivan's early work reflects Romanesque and even Art Nouveau qualities. His masterpiece is generally held to be the thoroughly functional Schlesinger-Mayer Store in Chicago (1899–1904). Frank Lloyd Wright trained in Sullivan's office.

Synagogue

A Jewish house of worship; originally the name of a female symbolic figure representing the Jewish Church beside the figure of 'Ecclesia' symbolizing Christendom.

Tablinum

Dining-room of a Roman house.

Tessenow, Heinrich (1876–1950)

A German architect who worked in the 'New Realism' but was not a strict adherent. He built principally dwelling-houses, also schools. Principal work: the garden city of Hellerau near Dresden with a festival theatre (1912).

Thermal baths

Roman designation for a warm bathing establishment usually consisting of a large hall with ante-rooms, Turkish bath, which were supplied with hot air through vents in the floor. The heating plant was subterranean.

Thersilium

Greek: a secular place of assembly.

Tholus

A Greek circular building with a columned ambulatory.

Three-apsed church

A basilica with three apses, one at the end of the choir and one at the end of each transept.

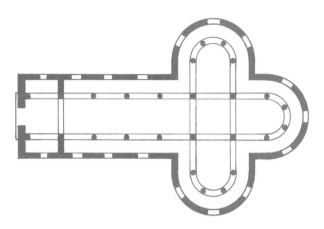

Tiepolo, Giovanni Battista (1696–1770)

An Italian painter, the most important fresco painter of the Baroque; worked in Venice, Vicenza, Udine, Würzburg, Madrid. Principal works: Villa Valmarana, Vicenza; Imperial Hall and Staircase in Würzburg; ceiling frescoes in Palazzo Labia in Venice.

Torus

The bulging base of a column.

Tower

A lofty building on a small ground area, free standing or built on or built up. The shape of the tower often allows one to see from afar the style of the building to which it belongs; but this may be deceptive, as the tower may have been built at a different period.

Tracery

With the exception of crabs (gable flowers) and cross flowers, almost all Gothic ornament is tracery, that is to say, it is measured with a compass, therefore it is constructed and abstract. A fish bladder is not so called because it was intended to represent a fish bladder, but because it has the appearance of one; the same is true of the clover leaf, the Flamboyant (flame-shaped) and Rayonnant (ray-shaped).

Transept

The part of a church which crosses the nave at right angles through an extension of the crossing. First employed in the basilica but at one end.

Trecento

(Italian 'three hundred'): in Italy and in Italian art the usual term for the fourteenth century.

Tribuna

An old term for 'apse'.

Triforium

An arcade usually under the windows of the church. In the Romanesque the triforium usually fills out the thickness of the wall; in the Gothic it usually corresponds to the thickness of the pillars. The significance of the triforium is more decorative than practical.

Triglyph (Greek: 'three holes')

A square field between the metopes in the entablature of a Doric temple with three perpendicular grooves. A rare variation is the tetraglyph with four grooves.

Trompe (French 'hunting horn')

A small half-domed arch in the upper corner of two walls, which makes an irregular octagon of the ceiling square; common in Islamic architecture.

Tudor arch (see 'Arch-forms')

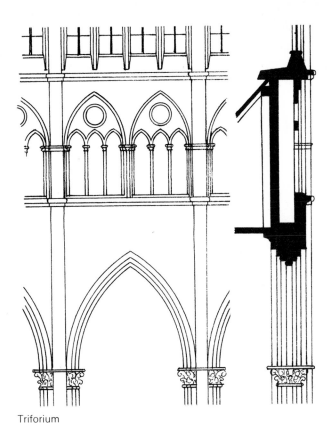

Triforium

Tunnel crypt

Burial-vault with tunnels branching off sideways for the reception of coffins. After the interment the tunnels were closed off by stones or by a memorial tablet.

Turret

Small decorative tower on the ridge of a gable roof.

Tympanum

The space above a doorway, circumscribed by the arch and the lintel.

179

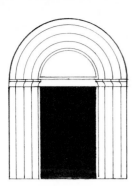
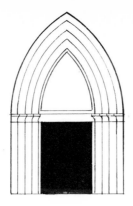

Vanbrugh, Sir John (1664–1726)
The outstanding English Baroque architect. Principal works: Blenheim Palace (1705–25); Castle Howard (1699); Seaton Delaval (1718); Grimsthorpe Castle (1723).

Vasari, Giorgio (1511–1574)
An Italian painter, architect and art historian; worked in Rome and Bologna. In 1564 he was architect to St Peter's. Principal works in Rome: Villa Papa Giulio, the smaller domes of St Peter's, Il Gesu church. Also palaces in Bologna and the palace of Caprarola near Viterbo. Author of an architectural textbook which became a signpost to the Baroque: *Regola delle cinque ordini dell'architettura*.

Vault
Arched roofing of a space, either in masonry or cast; massive, of uniform thickness or strengthened by ribs (ribbed vaulting), in which case the ribs bear the weight. In a genuine vault the seams (joints) are adjusted to the middle axis; in the so-called false vault they are horizontal.

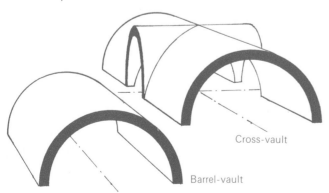

Cross-vault

Barrel-vault

Villard de Honnecourt
A French Gothic master of the thirteenth century. To him we owe the only book of the building guilds which has survived. (See the chapter 'Gothic'.)

Vitruvius Pollio
A Roman architect, author of the work *De Architectura* written in 25 B.C. and dedicated to the Emperor Augustus. Rediscovered in the fifteenth century, it became the authoritative manual for the architects of the Renaissance. In this book the three classical orders of columns are formulated.

Volute
A snake-line or S-shaped spiral; as a spiral it is the characteristic element of the Ionic capital. Volutes were used in the Middle Ages. They only appeared again in the high Renaissance and were of great significance in the Baroque.

Vulcanized cement
A fluid building material made of volcanic ash, rubble and water. (See 'Introduction'.)

Wedge-cut
The decoration of a surface or a frieze by regular wedge-shaped incisions: in wood with a veining tool, a V-shaped cutting iron; in stone with a chisel.

Welsh hood
Bell-shaped tower hood.

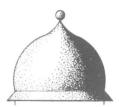

West front
The western cross building in front of the nave of the mediaeval church, accentuated architecturally by towers. (For details see the chapter 'Romanesque').

Window-sill
The lower, horizontal part of the window surround, usually sloping and slightly projecting.

Women's side
The northern side of a church interior, where the women sit separately from the men. This custom was strictly observed in the Middle Ages. The women's side is also the side from which the gospel is read.

Wren, Sir Christopher (1632–1723)
Architect of English Classicism with a Palladian tendency; worked in London. The great quantity of his work is a result of the Great Fire of London in 1666. Principal works: St Paul's Cathedral; St Stephen's, Walbrook; Greenwich Hospital; the east wing of Hampton Court Palace; the Great Fire Memorial.

Wright, Frank Lloyd (1867 or 1869–1959)
An American architect, pupil of Sullivan. Fundamentally new ideas for dwelling-houses and public buildings. Principal works: 'Prairie houses'; Fallingwater dwelling-house in Pennsylvania 1936; Guggenheim Museum in New York 1959 (designed in 1946).

Yevele, Henry (c. 1353–1400)
The outstanding architect of the English Perpendicular style. Yevele was eminent as a military, a civil and as an ecclesiastical designer. Principal works include Westminster Hall (1394–9); Canterbury Cathedral Nave (1391–1400); Southwark Cathedral Tower (c. 1400).

Zimmermann, Dominikus (1685–1766)
A Baroque architect working in Swabia and in upper Bavaria; creator of numerous small village churches, in which he adopts a cheerful style which is typical of his work. Principal works: the pilgrimage church at Steinhausen; the Frauenkirche (church of Our Lady) at Gunzburg; the pilgrimage church at Wies near Steingaden.

Egyptian picture sign for 'Many thousand years'

Chronological Charts

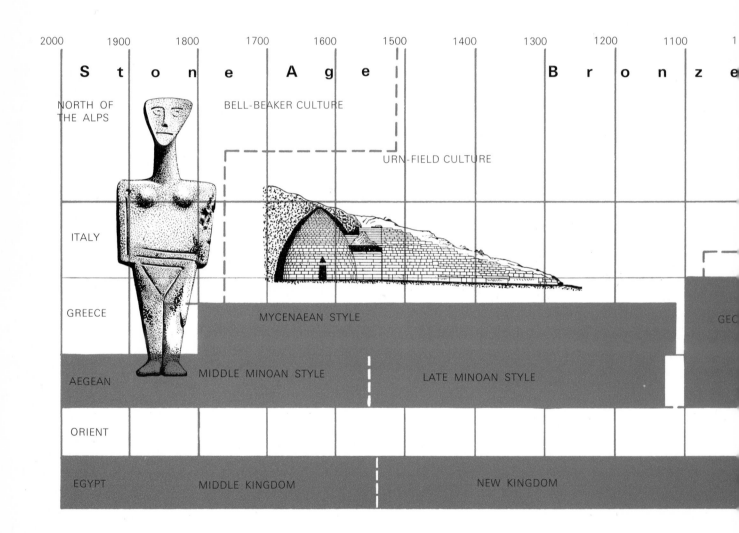

2000	1900	1800	1700	1600	1500	1400	1300	1200	1100	

S t o n e A g e **B r o n z e**

NORTH OF
THE ALPS   BELL-BEAKER CULTURE

URN-FIELD CULTURE

ITALY

GREECE   MYCENAEAN STYLE   GEO

AEGEAN   MIDDLE MINOAN STYLE   LATE MINOAN STYLE

ORIENT

EGYPT   MIDDLE KINGDOM   NEW KINGDOM

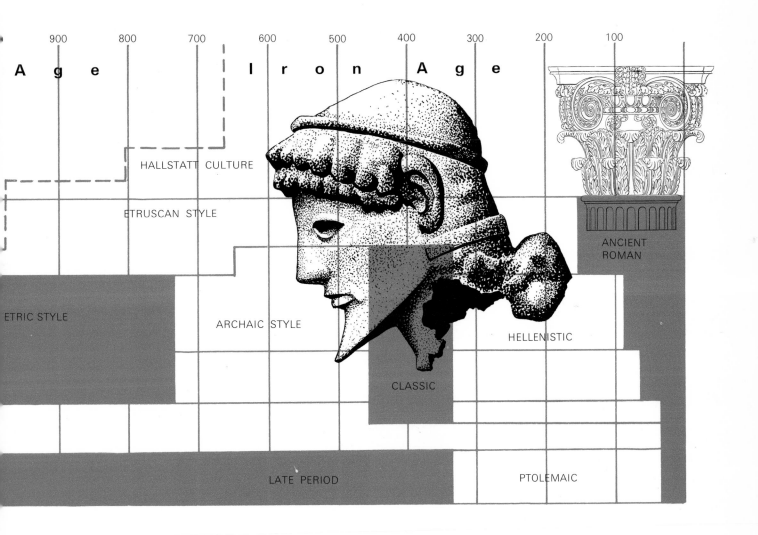

900   800   700   600   500   400   300   200   100

A g e   I r o n   A g e

HALLSTATT CULTURE

ETRUSCAN STYLE

ANCIENT
ROMAN

ETRIC STYLE

ARCHAIC STYLE

HELLENISTIC

CLASSIC

LATE PERIOD

PTOLEMAIC

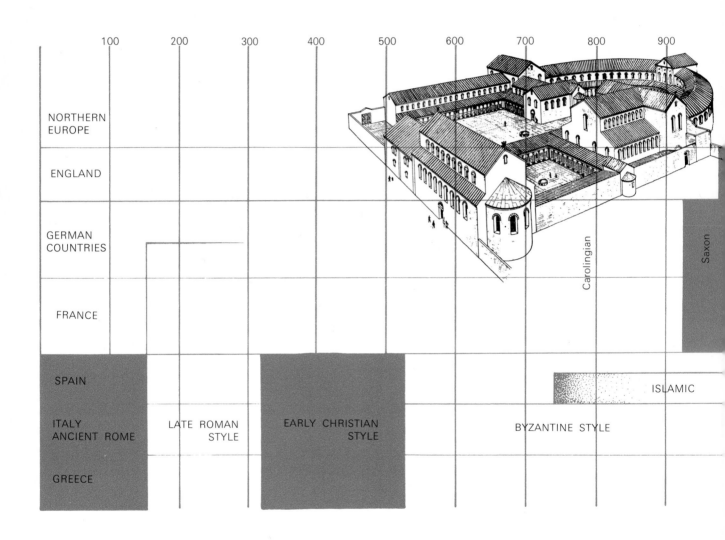

	100	200	300	400	500	600	700	800	900
NORTHERN EUROPE									
ENGLAND									
GERMAN COUNTRIES									
FRANCE									
SPAIN									ISLAMIC
ITALY ANCIENT ROME	LATE ROMAN STYLE			EARLY CHRISTIAN STYLE		BYZANTINE STYLE			
GREECE									

Carolingian

Saxon

186

1100   1200   1300   1400   1500   1600   1700   1800   1900

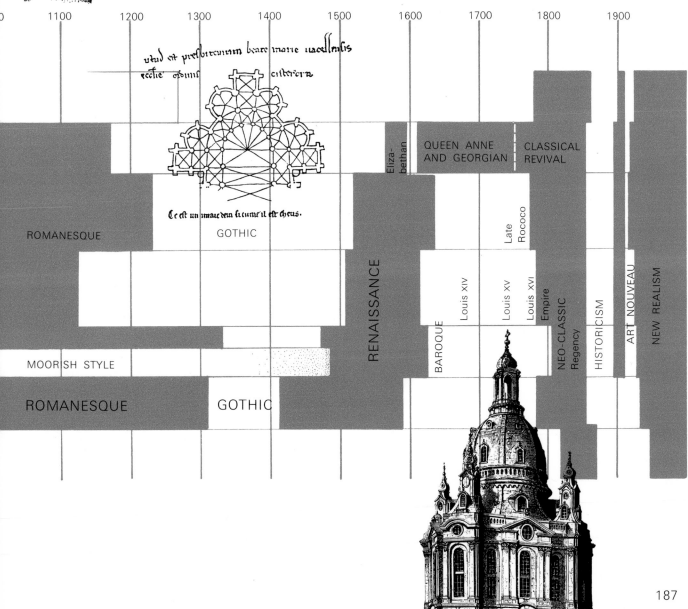

utud est presbiterium beare marie nacellensis
ecclie ordinis cisterciensis

Ce est un image dein si cumeril est cheus.

GOTHIC

ROMANESQUE

Elizabethan

QUEEN ANNE AND GEORGIAN

CLASSICAL REVIVAL

Late Rococo

RENAISSANCE

Louis XIV

Louis XV

Louis XVI

Empire

NEO-CLASSIC

Regency

HISTORICISM

ART NOUVEAU

NEW REALISM

BAROQUE

MOORISH STYLE

ROMANESQUE

GOTHIC